STUDENT OF THE UNIVERSE

FROM ROCK N' ROLL SINGER TO PSYCHIC MEDIUM

DOC O'TOOLE

BALBOA.PRESS

A DIVISION OF HAY HOUSE

Balboa Press books may be ordered through booksellers or by contacting:

Balboa Press
A Division of Hay House
1663 Liberty Drive
Bloomington, IN 47403
www.balboapress.com.au
1 (877) 407-4847

Print information available on the last page.

ISBN: 978-1-5043-2095-5 (sc)
ISBN: 978-1-5043-2096-2 (e)

Balboa Press rev. date: 03/03/2020

CONTENTS

DEDICATION

Karen Geraghty
24/07/1947–09/09/2018

This book is dedicated to a wonderful, caring, kind, loving, and selfless woman who made an impact on all who were privileged to come into contact with her. A strong woman, Karen was there, tirelessly and selflessly, for all who needed her, throughout her lifetime. Karen will always be fondly remembered by her family, friends, and associates.

Thanking you for all your love, support and kindness.

INTRODUCTION

Writing this book has been a considerable undertaking. I never thought that I would be writing a book, which came to me through a series of divine promptings, which showed me, without a doubt, that this was to be a part of what I was to do in this lifetime. From the very beginning of my journey, many people showed up along my pathway to offer encouragement and support, keeping me on track, advancing me to this completed result. Within the book, I write about stepping outside your comfort zone. Well, I have indeed done that.

It was a chance meeting with a medium during a meal, overlooking the Atlantic Ocean that set me on this journey. During a very general conversation, the medium, who I will call Joy, suddenly switched the discussion. Within the next breath, she said to me, "You have to write books." It took me a few seconds to readjust my thoughts from a general conversation to now one of mediumship. Caught quite by surprise, I quickly realised that Joy had been chosen to deliver me a message from Spirit. I said to Joy, "Books? Plural?" I sat there in amazement, looking back and forth between Joy and the figure who now appeared beside her.

There had been a prominent figure whom I saw quite clearly standing next to Joy, who had passed away a few years before, as she was giving me a reading that day, which intensely validated what she had been conveying. I was absolutely floored with whom I was seeing, as I put down my knife and fork to negotiate within my mind what was now suddenly taking place. I had mentioned to Joy a few times throughout the impromptu reading as I sat there in amazement, "Do you know who is standing next to you?" I also mentioned the name of the person standing there, but Joy, as it seemed, never heard a word that I said. Thus began the first step towards writing this book.

I had begun to write a journal in January 2016 after a funny incident had taken place. Karen, to whom I have dedicated this book, had been very concerned about my health, as I was under pressure to complete a painting contract. I had been working fifteen-hour days, seven days a week, as I had yet again been pushing myself to the limits. Karen had said to me on this Friday, "You're not going to be working tonight, are you?" I knew that I was going to be working late, but responded, "No, I'll be finishing early." Well, it seems that Spirit had other plans, as at 5:00 p.m. on the dot, I leaned over to pour paint into my roller tray, and as I did this, my phone slid out of my top pocket and into the paint, fully submerging, in slow motion, into the abyss of the paint tray. I quickly and calmly retrieved my now "Antique White USA"–coloured phone from the depths of the paint tray and very calmly proceeded to wash and try to save my freshly painted communication apparatus. Instantly, I knew what had divinely taken place. Reading the signs that I had to take a break, I packed up and had an early day, along with a well-deserved rest.

The following day, I headed to the shopping centre to renew my phone with my mobile phone provider. As you may know, it can take ages to be served at these types of stores. However, it was as if I was greeted with the red carpet treatment, as I was attended to straight away, with ease. As I explained to the manager what had happened to my phone, I noticed her holding back her laughter. I thought, *She shares my sense of humour!* The young lady could not have been more helpful. I had my new mobile phone, and with the next breath, the young lady in the store said, "This is also for you" as she handed me a writing tablet as a bonus.

Within a half-hour of entering the department store, I was heading home with my purchase in hand, still laughing about the whole ordeal while at the same time amazed at the orchestration of Spirit. Later that day, I began to write about the "painted phone incident," which for most people would have freaked them out, but for me, it had hit my funny bone. After finishing the journal that day, I thought it would be nice to get a protective cover for my new writing tablet, so I headed back to the store. On arrival, I realised that no one had remembered or recognised me. In fact, I seemed to be invisible to those within the store.

As I waited and scanned around the department store, I noticed a huge white feather on the floor of where I was standing. Grinning to myself, I knew that this was a sign from my spirit guides, and I very quickly realised what had taken place, understanding why the "painted phone incident" had happened. How often do you find a huge white feather in a department store? It was definitely a sign to begin writing. So I quietly left the store and headed back home.

Spirit can be brilliant at orchestrating events. I'm always amazed at how the divine energies gain our attention. All we have to do is listen. Spirit had wrapped my lesson and my new life direction all up into one neat package. So I began, slowly, to write a book. When I say slowly, I mean *slowly*. By the time I had met Joy, the medium, more than twelve months later, I had a title, I had written a page, and then I clicked the save button. My life had changed that day when Joy passed the mediumistic message on to me, to then attending my first Hay House Writer's Workshop a few months later.

At the Hay House Writer's Workshop in Sydney a month after my impromptu reading, I was in the foyer walking around looking at all the stands of books that were on display. I happened upon Balboa Press, who at that time, I knew little to nothing about. They invited me to be on their mailing list. I said, "Sure, why not?"

That following September, after the Hay House Writer's Workshop, I received a phone call from Balboa Press, asking what my book was about. Thinking on my feet, I went on to discuss my thoughts about what I would like to write about for the benefit of mankind. One hour later, I was signed to Balboa Press.

What kept me going throughout my journey of writing was that it's not about me, and it's not about the book. It's about you, the reader, who may gain insights into your own lives as you navigate through my writings.

PROLOGUE

We are all energy. Energy is everywhere. Energy is all around us. Energy, though it cannot be destroyed, it can be transformed.

This book is a collection of situations and experiences that I have personally witnessed throughout my lifetime. I had been writing in my journal about a funny incident that happened to me recently when I began to then realise that my journal was actually a chapter in a book that I was to write. I also remembered that the divine energies had been prompting me to write this book for a while.

This made sense to me as I listened to my own stories and thoughts within my mind during that coming week. I've always shared my stories with those willing to listen, and with those whom I meet in my travels, with the hope that they may too gain insight and direction in their lives.

As you read this book, you will notice that my stories are not of the typical day to day life—or for you, maybe they are. I will share with you my metaphors, symbologies, signs, and visions. As far back as I can remember, I have always had a deeper understanding and a different kind of knowing.

I was always the different one. Yes, I was called weird and strange, but luckily, this was most positively. I really didn't know or understand what this was all about—being a psychic and now a medium? Me? Not me. I'm not like that. I can't do that!

At times, I would be helping people with daily situations, while at other times, I would perform readings with accuracy, but I never believed or recognised my God-given abilities. That realisation would come to me much later on in life, when I would acknowledge and own my gifts and skills with pride, becoming of service to mankind, using my abilities in a more structured way.

Remembering when I first saw John Edward on his TV show, *Crossing Over, with John Edward*, back in 2001, right from the start of the series, I was hooked, addicted to watching his every appearance. At that time, I had no idea what a psychic medium was or how John Edward was so accurate with the messages he was delivering to his audience members. But somehow, I knew, 100 percent, that he was the real deal with whatever it was that he was doing. As many of us witnessed watching his show, so many lives were being positively transformed.

It would not be for quite a few more years that I became totally involved with metaphysics. In fact, it took another nine years until I owned my abilities. It's quite hard to explain how I discovered and used my abilities, being of service helping others in the past yet at the same time, never genuinely acknowledging my abilities. I often am bamboozled myself at the thought process. I sometimes have a laugh on reflection, thinking, *How would one explain this type of quandary to another?*

I found myself in a total state of perplexity. It was like living as two different people at one time. One explanation for not acknowledging it would be that for the past thirty years, I had been totally fixated on my singing career. Sometimes while on stage, I would witness an audience member going through a hard time, so I would focus my energies towards them, singing a particular line from a song and pushing my energies out to them with the hope of delivering a healing message. Another thing I would do with my energy (which I now know to be my *auric field*) was to push my energy out, shielding me before taking the stage to not become swamped with questions from punters, keeping people at bay so I could prepare myself mentally while staying focused for the show that night. I was always polite, but I was usually looking for an exit point during the conversation. I will write more on this energy later.

These days, as I am now in full swing and using my abilities to help people, I wouldn't have it any other way. I have now dedicated my life to helping people with my abilities, using a range of modalities, working weekends, in the evenings, or after work.

After around 2011, life began to change for me. The music industry was getting me down, and a good friend passed from cancer, which really rocked my world. Rhonda—or Ronnie, as I called her—was definitely an angel living among us. Well, that's how I saw her. She was always there totally unconditionally, being of service to those in need. Whether it was donating her time and spending it with the homeless at Christmas time while giving out Christmas gifts or putting a roof over someone in need of somewhere to live, she was always helping.

I spoke with Ronnie one night as she was dealing so bravely with her illness to see how she was. She would always respond positively, saying, "I am fine." One night during our conversation, she asked me if a particular guitarist had contacted me. Curiously, I said, "No, why would he be contacting me?" To my absolute amazement, as sick as she was, Ronnie had been looking for a guitarist for my band. I couldn't believe that a person with stage-four cancer could even have the strength to so selflessly care of others. This is one of many good stories about her.

Ronnie's passing took the wind out of my sails, transforming my life forever, as I very much realised how fragile we indeed all are. Looking back on that period of my life, I can see that Spirit was getting me ready for my life's purpose. "Now is the time," I imagine them saying.

Soon after Ronnie's passing, a dear friend, Karen, began to become very inquisitive about metaphysics, always questioning me about the afterlife, along with the questions like "What is an angel?" It had been a long time since I had really been involved with conducting readings, meditating, and, as I know it now, "mediumistic" work.

Two years previously, my good friend Caroline, whom I had known for many years, was no stranger to my spiritual ways. While living in England with her husband, Ty, Caroline had felt the need to send me a pack of Archangel Rafael oracle cards, which was very thoughtful, indeed.

The cards sat on my desk for two years, until that day, Karen expressed curiosity about my spiritual side. Spirit was on a mission and really preparing me to start my work, placing situations on my pathway and therefore kickstarting me back onto my metaphysical journey, full-time. The way that I view it now, it was the way for Spirit to push me forward onto my new path, putting my life-changing situation into the hands of both Caroline and Karen—along with another crucial person in the future, Sonja.

It had been a little harsh in the beginning trying to remember the answers to the metaphysical question asked of me. I had to oil the cogs of my mind to retrieve the knowledge buried deep within. I'm so glad I listened to Spirit—not to mention very thankful to both Carolyn and the persistent questioning of Karen. The third person to set me on my way would be Sonja, who at that time was part owner of Krystal Kamali.

I had gone through a lot over the past few years. We all go through hard times throughout our lives, as you may have also experienced. However, if we hang in there, we learn and evolve to a higher level of understanding. It seemed to me that my world was falling apart. Everything was changing, and I couldn't understand why. I really didn't feel that I was a part of anything or anyone anymore. However, my friends couldn't see what the problem was, as I didn't know how to explain what I was experiencing. I was in a depressed state of mind for a long while. To this day, I am amazed at how I operated and kept on venturing forward. There had been a nudging feeling within me, pushing me forward, with the understanding that the nudging feeling had been coming from a higher source.

I remembered that I had periodically always seen blue flashes. For years, I tried finding out what this was all about. The doctors curiously looked at me, wondering what I meant when I asked about the blue flashes. Optometrists had no idea either. Still transitioning through my depression, I finally started to see through the mist of foggy cloud that had surrounded me for a long while, as I finally began to see the blue sky once again.

A feeling came over me to start researching the blue flashes I had seen for many years. Quite by accident, I happened upon an article through an Internet search, which led me to believe that the blue flashes indicated the presence of the Archangel Michael. I had no way of truly knowing if this was the case, though I had the secure knowledge that this was the answer for which I had been searching. I was unsure how I knew that Michael was there to be of divine assistance. Trusting this newfound knowledge, I began to ask Archangel Michael for help and direction. As I did, I started to feel better and started to heal. I began meditating daily and have done so ever since that night of discovery, when a new world opened up around me.

Finally, I was on the road to full health. As I was thinking of the need to better my situation, a strong urge came over me to have a reiki session, which I knew very little about at the time. I found a reiki master and booked an appointment for that afternoon.

Having reiki performed on me was the best move I had ever made in my life up to that point. I was lucky enough to find an advanced reiki healer. The Reiki session that I experienced that afternoon was unexplainable and the best thing I had ever witnessed. I was visited by angels and past loved ones during my session, as I further saw a large circular, solid-gold doorway. I'm not sure was the door was all about, which I am still yet to understand. On the other side of the solid gold doorway, it was pitch black. I felt that there was a choice to either enter this doorway or to stay on this side.

For the first time in a few years, I was finally feeling like part of the human race once again. Although I still had a long way to go, my inner strength and inner peace were beginning to return, as if I had evolved to a new level within my life. I was so fascinated by the reiki treatment performed on me that I, one day, decided I wanted to become a reiki master to help people and to be of service in this way.

I knew that I was a healer. I had been helping people for many years. I guess that starting to own my abilities and being a healer was only one part of me. My clairvoyant visions, clairaudients, and clairsentient skills began to grow stronger as I began to start seeing my life's purpose for the first time. As I look back now, I have had these abilities for as long as I can remember. As I mentioned earlier, I didn't acknowledge them and didn't see that I could be doing metaphysical work in a more structured way.

Back in the early 1990s, Spirit had been giving me a taste of all that I was capable of. I'd hear my name called out when there was no one around (known as a *disembodied voice*). I also found that I had the knowledge of how to astral travel—by "just knowing" without any formal training. If you are unfamiliar with astral travel, it's known as an intentional out-of-body experience -(OBE). These and other blessings had been placed among my many metaphysical experiences. I had received no formal training in any of the spiritual modalities. At times, I would perform readings for people, using tarot cards, with about 90 percent accuracy. I'd also dream of situations that came true, and I received an introduction to mental telepathy. The list of experiences seemed endless. It was a fantastic time, granting me the knowledge that I hold dearly. I had no idea what all these experiences were about until I began working and studying metaphysics. Now I know the names, titles, and meanings of the different clairs.

Cues Studios was a rehearsal studio where I would spend a lot of time rehearsing; occasionally, I would also work there. One evening, a friend and part-owner, Daniel, and I were having a conversation about psychic abilities—this was a typical dialogue between Daniel and myself. On one occasion, Daniel gave me a gift of old French tarot cards. He said, knowingly, "These are for you. You will make better use of them than me."

Unbeknownst to me, Daniel was right. I used these cards soon after to do an occasional one-on-one reading for friends, with high accuracy. The funny thing about my abilities back then was that I didn't think much of them. It was like, *Wow, that's cool.* My next thought might then be *What's for dinner?* There was a period, also around this time, that clairvoyants were becoming friends. Following some suggestions that I start reading tarot, I'd reply, "I'm not like that. I can't do that type of work!"

Travelling to a friend's home, about an hour or so south of Sydney, where I was living at the time, I was asked by my friend's partner if I would perform a reading for her. I obliged while remembering that my friend Mac was a nonbeliever.

I set up the reading in a quiet, low-lit atmosphere and began the reading without the use of tarot cards. Quietly taking deep breaths to relax, I began to see video footage within my mind. As I sat there feeling very relaxed, I was watching footage of scenes that were appearing in and around the sitter's life. I watched a situation where a relative of the sitter was receiving a parcel that was being delivered. Within the package was an award for a course that her sister had passed a week or so previously. At one stage during the reading, I looked up at Mac, who was a sceptic, and I noticed his amazed look. I thought, *Well, it looks like I'm doing something right here. I'll keep going.*

I explained the outlay of the home that I had seen, describing the gate that the sitters relative had walked through to get to her front door, along with a description of the house in which her relative lived in. At the end of the reading, I went about my typical visit as if this reading hadn't actually occurred. There was more to that reading, but mostly, I don't remember much of that evening. After this particular night, it would be at least another twenty years before I owned my abilities.

Today, with what I now know and understand as a working psychic medium, I have been operating in the early stages in an area that I knew nothing about, although there had been an internally secure knowing. It's quite incredible once you own your abilities and then start to look back on certain happenings in your lifetime. Like you, I'm here on earth for a specific reason, which is to be of service to mankind. Whether you are a beautician beautifying someone for their first time or helping the elderly and disadvantaged along their way, we all have a purpose.

Reiki had captured my interest, so I set out in search of classes with a mind to becoming a reiki master. I found a few local teachers who were charging a ridiculous amount for Reiki One. The reiki classes that seemed legit at the right price were a few hours away from where I lived, which made it tricky. However, if I had to drive a long way to do the course, then that's what I would do. I was prepared to do what it took to achieve this outcome.

In the following weeks, I met a tradesman named Shannon on a job site. It was a Saturday morning as I arrived on-site, greeted by both Shannon and his dad, who were on-site laying carpet in the home, which I had been re-painting for a friend.

Right from the word go, Shannon started talking with me. Very quickly, the conversation proceeded to metaphysics. He mentioned that he had just completed his second module for reiki. Shannon had these incredible blue eyes that reminded me of the archangel Michael, so he had my attention from the get-go. Knowing that this chance meeting was for a reason, the conversation led Shannon to mention a new crystal shop called Krystal Kamali, which had recently opened up nearby. We spoke for at least four hours that day; it cost me a half a day's work, but it was well worth it.

I went to Krystal Kamali a few times after Shannon introduced me to the new store. One day, I had a feeling, and I was prompted to go and have a meeting with one of the owners, Sonja, to pick her brain. I arrived at Krystal Kamali on a Wednesday around lunchtime to have a general meeting with Sonja. She had been reading tarot and platforming for many years, and she was well versed in her abilities.

Sitting in the front reading room, talking about reiki (among other topics I can't seem to recall), out of nowhere, Sonja said, "You start reading here in a fortnight." She said in a very Sonja way, "My guides just slapped me in the back of the head and said, 'Hire him.' You start reading here in a fortnight, and you will be doing fifteen-minute readings."

"Fifteen-minute readings?" I replied. "Are you sure? Fifteen minutes isn't long enough for a reading!"

Sonja said, "Okay before you start, I want you to do a reading for me."

"Fair enough," I said. "I'll be back here at 2:00 p.m. tomorrow to perform a reading for you."

I arrived at Krystal Kamali the next day, as scheduled. I was in the kitchen, making myself a cup of coffee as I began picking up on Sonja regarding cats.

Okay, Doc, I said to myself, *here we go. Have faith and trust in the messages that you are receiving.*

I began the reading for Sonja. I mentioned that I was actively picking up on cats around her. "What does this mean to you?" I asked.

Sonja replied, "I love my cats" as she pointed to a shelf behind me, which had a display of statues in the shape of small black cats.

I thought, *Wow, this is unbelievable!* At the same time, I could feel my confidence building as I relaxed into the reading. I began my favourite five-card tarot spread. The spread was left to right—distant past, immediate past, present, immediate future, and distant future. In no time, I had the reading table full of tarot cards. I was flowing as if I'd been doing this for many years.

Suddenly, Sonja said, "You know that you are a half-hour over time?"

I replied, "That's okay. It's for you!"

Sonja was very pleased with the reading I had done, which was a big compliment coming from her. She said, "You won't be doing fifteen-minute readings. You'll be doing one-hour readings."

I was so excited as I began to realise, with a sense of validation, what my journey was to be while at the same time recognising what Spirit had been directing me to do all those years ago. Spirit finally had my attention, and I was now switched on and listening.

CHAPTER 1
BIRDS WITHOUT A SONG

Stop. Breathe. Think. Act. Then you may continue.

We tend to travel through our lives, doing what we love to do. You may have wanted to be a rock star—like yours truly—or maybe a nurse, doctor, or landscape gardener. Inherently, we may start out in our lives and careers following what we see as our gravitational directional pull. We spend lots of time with years of study and commitment building our lives, our futures, and our hopes and dreams— giving us a direction in life, along with the strength and courage to keep moving forward in order to succeed. By following our feelings and passions, we are true to ourselves; it's what we should be doing as we begin our journey through life. We all have to start somewhere, and as we do, it's with positivity, passion, and direction. We do this with blind enthusiasm, not stopping to think that our lives have a starting position and a finishing position, just like every living thing on this planet. That type of innocence is a beautiful blessing bestowed upon us all.

Imagine going on a road trip for a week, with your destination all mapped out. You even have a vision in your mind of the way the road trip should be. So you start out on your adventure, feeling free for the first time in many years, travelling without a strict itinerary and stopping when you feel like it. You are literally feeling the stress of the past days and months—working nine to five, year after year—peel away from your mind, body, and soul. This provokes a forgotten feeling of freedom that envelops you.

All of a sudden, there is a detour ahead of you, due to planned road works. You must take the unfamiliar detour road that now lies ahead of you. At first, your stress levels and fear of the unknown resurface as you become afraid of the unknown that lies ahead. The favourite song that is pumping out of your car stereo seems now to annoy you, transitioning into white noise. You pause your favourite CD, which is digitally orchestrated at a comfortable volume through the audio speakers so that in silence, you can then feel out the new journey ahead of you.

Driving along the new highway is likened to the highway of life. They both have detours, potholes in the roads, obstacles across your path, and dead ends.

Life Is a Highway

Detours. The universe is always trying to get your attention. All we need to do is to listen to the silence and its surroundings.

If you stop, breathe, think, and act, you will be able to hear, see, feel, and do to gain an understanding of your life's purpose. There is nothing to be afraid of. Some people do fear the unknown—until they realise that change is a natural life progression.

Stepping outside your comfort zone is a big deal for a lot of us, although it is incredible when we do venture out from our comfortable lifestyles. It can be life-changing and rewarding, to say the least. I have personally found that when stepping out to own my gifts and abilities, if I don't listen and place faith in God, my spirit guides, and the Archangel Michael, which are my beliefs and faith, I will tend to learn the hard way. Fortunately, this is not as often these days as I am more in tune with my surroundings.

I have always been blown away with how the universe works. It is absolutely incredible. A detour is not a negative. It is a positive change in our lives. If you think about a significant change in your life that has transitioned in the past, it didn't seem much fun going through it until you saw the whole scenario, after the transition.

By keeping an open mind and being in tune with what you see, hear, and feel, while walking in humble, silent steps, you will see why certain situations happen in your life. Sometimes you can't see and are not meant to know until you reflect on the circumstances and piece it all together while looking at the steps that led you to the place that is now. It's incredible when we stop and look back at those essential steps while gazing at where we are now. I'm always grateful and amazed at how the universal energies work. You may even find yourself laughing out loud, as I sometimes do, as you stop to take stock of your journey.

Potholes. There are always bumps and holes in the road. They teach us to think outside the square, to overcome obstacles and adapt to certain situations. Sometimes it's a wake-up call, showing you that your circumstances aren't really as unfortunate as they may seem. There are always people worse off in the world than you or me who would benefit significantly with generosity and help in their times of need. This, in turn, could point out your life's purpose or reveal a new direction for you.

Getting used to reading and understanding daily signs and symbols can help significantly throughout your lifetime. Everybody has their own personal signs, so it is good practice to start a journal relating to what your personal signs are and their meanings.

One way to look at a question that you may have is something that I say to people when they ask me, "How do I listen? How do I understand what a sign is?" In truth, it takes a lot of practice and fine-tuning, but the best advice is to start by taking it one step at a time. However, to get people to begin to understand themselves, and to ensure they start listening to their own bodies, I ask them, "How do you know when to drink water?" They are amazed when they hear my answer, which is "Your body tells you." Listen to your body, and respond by having a glass of water. It's the same with hunger or tiredness. Your body tells you to eat or sleep.

People are amazed as they realise that they already knew the answer but never stopped to think about it. Why should they think about it? It's all there working, naturally, from the time of birth. It's second nature, the same as breathing is a natural perpetual motion. However, you definitely begin to appreciate and understand the body's workings if you start to have trouble breathing!

Take a few minutes to think about your body and how it works day after day. We don't "plug in" each night; we go to bed to charge up our internal power source. Sleep and rest take care of that. Have you ever zoned out and watched your feet, ankles, knees, and legs as you walked, one step after the other, along the seashore? The human body is quite an amazing creation that is attuned for our day-to-day existence, which we tend to sometimes take for granted.

Obstacles. Have you heard the saying "overcome and adapt"? What a classic phrase!

That is an impactful phrase that contains power and gusto to get you moving to make a difference in your endeavours. You begin looking at obstacles as puzzles instead of problems to be solved, and you start looking at situations in a much more positive way. You receive the strength to pick yourself up and to deal with the circumstances that enter your life throughout your time here on earth.

There are many problems to be solved. It's not a one-time occurrence. It's a lifetime of evolution within ourselves. You may not immediately deal with a type of problem or situation, but in saying to yourself, "Overcome and adapt," and really coming to understand the meaning of this phrase, you will have acknowledged the problem. You will have then planted a seed within your mind to solve the puzzle at hand. In truth, you have put the universal laws of attraction into motion, creating a solution to move forward.

You will find that over the following days, you will be thinking about how to rectify a situation. Most of the time, the puzzles that you have—that need to be solved—will come up in life situations and conversations, leading you to a solution.

People around you have already dealt with the same problems or situations that you may be dealing with. Their job is to shine some of their light and knowledge on your situation to help you to evolve within your life. In a way, this is related to the butterfly effect. For example, one day, you too will be helping someone, somewhere, with a problem or puzzling situation that you have had the privilege of solving for yourself while sharing your knowledge to be of assistance.

We are also born with free will. By asking for divine help for your situation from your higher sources, you will generate positive outcomes and resolutions. Believe and trust in the divine energies, knowing that support is on its way when you ask for it. And yes, you must ask. Remember, we are born with free will. The divine sources, whether they be God, your spirit guides, angels, or whatever your faith may be, have your permission to give you support, help, and guidance. They are only too happy and never too busy to be of assistance. They are always waiting for you to ask for their support.

However, help does not always come in the way that you expect. When you expect something to happen in a certain direct way, you cancel out any other possibilities of the universe helping you. This means that you are trying to control the outcome instead of *letting go and letting God*. Thus, disappointment will set in, and your faith will dissipate, leaving you to build yourself and your confidence back up again over time. This will make you stronger and wiser in the long run. We can only learn from these events. There's no wrong or right way, only lessons learned together with a new depth of understanding. When we learn, we advance within ourselves, so it's a win-win situation.

Dead Ends. Trust, believe and strive to be the best that you possibly can be, with the gifts and abilities you were born with. As we evolve, we learn lessons, arriving at an understanding of our life's purpose. That, in itself, is a new kind of freedom.

Helping others less fortunate than you is one way of understanding what your life's purpose is. You can be a successful person or a spiritually successful person—spiritually successful is what I prefer because that is giving back, paying forward, and helping your fellow man.

A dead-end can mean that you have come to the end of a chapter in your life and that you have earned the right to rise to the next level. You can only achieve this by committing 100 percent in all that you do. Yes, we take a few steps forward and one step back, but achievement is the ultimate result.

Metaphorically speaking, what do you do in a situation when you hit a dead-end or a brick wall or a locked door? The answer is that you find a way to punch through to that next level. Climb over or go through the brick wall, or if the door is locked, go through the window or simply call a locksmith. You can phone a friend or research ways around the issues at hand; in other words, give it your best shot, and never be too proud to ask for help. While you are here on this earth, you might as well get busy living.

A close friend, John, is always saying, "Make it take it." He has recently taken a leap of faith, resigning from his comfortable, secure job to create a business working with his passion, beekeeping. Because of his positivity, he attracts and surrounds himself with positive support, from his friends and family to those that he meets as clients to casual associates. As John believes and backs himself, those who are associated with him come to believe in his new venture and in his passions, in turn offering encouragement and support for him as he produces the healthy production of natural honey. Remember, positive energies attract positive energies; on the contrary, negative energies attract negative energies. We become who we are by what we think.

John, who is one of the most positive people I've met, hit a "dead end." Life as a truck salesman wasn't fulfilling his internal needs. Eventually, he jumped ship and decided to do something about it by taking a giant leap of faith. He now has his business up and running—very successfully, I might add.

It wasn't easy for him at all. However, faith, determination, and hard work have brought him to his current position in life. It takes a lot of hard work, dedication, and faith to have the courage to move forward. John arrived at a point in his life where he had no choice but to answer his calling, by surrendering to that nudging feeling from within, as he did. Taking the bull by the horns and having the courage to step outside of his comfort zone landed positive results for John while leading him on a journey of self-discovery.

That calling is within each and every one of us. Fear stops us from moving forward but always remember: love gives us the courage to conquer fear. When you feel that fear, which is "energy" eager to go somewhere, try to redirect that fear-energy and direct it straight into positive energy. For example, if you become "angry-energy" for any reason, hearing *ding ding ding* as you come out swinging, stop, breathe, think, act, and then try transferring that negative energy into positive energy, perhaps by performing ten or twenty pushups. This way, you are diverting the negative energies into positive energy.

These written guidelines above will help you travel on the new road that you were detoured to. With practice and time, you will become comfortable in your new highway of life while taking in the sights, smells, and sounds. Eventually, you will become very comfortable as you zoom forward on your new road. Over time, you will make the new road, along with many other new roads, a part of your personal life's journey, feeding your onboard wisdom toolbox with invaluable gathered knowledge.

You've now turned on the music within, cranking the volume way up to eleven while noticing that you're now vibrating with renewed positivity and enthusiasm. Your mind is tirelessly thinking of all the things you want to achieve in life. You become a bird in flight, soaring through the skies over the deep blue ocean. You are no longer a bird without a song. You have become the loudest, most melodic bird in the glistening morning sun. You begin to attract other positive people around you, bringing new opportunities, filling your sails with the trade winds as you ride the backs of every white horse, rolling and splashing to the sandy shorelines.

Yin and yang, balance, negative/positive—one cannot operate without the strength of the other. We all love to be happy and joyful, living life without a care. In reality, this is not always possible. We are human, and we can get down in the mouth at times, withdrawing from the world. Hopefully, you will gain insight and tools from my book so that you can pick yourself up and dust yourself off, continuing forward with a more productive way of thinking. It's a choice—you can choose between being a victim or victor, sad or happy, lover or hater. Being happy and content is the ultimate choice of outcome to achieve; it isn't always easy, but it is very possible. Sometimes we have to change the way we look at a situation so that we can positively reframe life's circumstances.

Remember, we are souls experiencing a human life, so don't be too hard on yourself. We are all here to evolve, to help others, and to learn via life's lessons.

Try looking at life in a positive light, no matter how you are feeling. We are all at fault for dwelling on the negative side of the coin. Negativity inevitably weighs you down, at times becoming a heavy load to carry around.

Why do we do this to ourselves? A few years ago, I overheard a conversation in a store. A friend of mine, Jack (not his real name), who, by the way, is a really great guy, jokingly brought me into the conversation that he was having with another. He said, "Doc, yeah he wouldn't work in an iron lung!" This grabbed my attention, as was his real purpose.

I replied, "You're absolutely 100 percent right! I wouldn't work in an iron lung. One thing, it's very cramped, and I am claustrophobic, and besides, have you ever smelled an iron lung in the blistering heat of the sun? No, I couldn't stomach that at all, so you are right: I wouldn't work in an iron lung, but I would work in the beautiful sunshine on a calm summers day."

The look on Jack's face was priceless. With his mouth open, he eventually said, "Thanks for that, Doc!"

I replied, "You're welcome, Jack. Have a prosperous day." Then I continued on my way, laughing.

Yes, indeed, Jack was only joking and giving me a ribbing, which I don't mind at all. However, you will often encounter situations where people unknowingly attempt to steal your energy in order to feed their own ego. For empaths, this can cause them to have a down day if they aren't already. If an empath doesn't understand that they are an empath, such remarks can cause self-doubt and put them out of action for a few days. As an empath, I have a hold of my sensitivity while being quick-witted. I can control the situation in a nice way while keeping my energy intact, a skill I have developed over many years.

"Birds without a song" are what you become if you lay down and accept what is dished out to you. Working in a job that you don't like because of the fear of not being able to support yourself or your family is not living. If you hate your job, I guarantee that someone else would absolutely love it. So, in saying that, don't you think that it is very possible for you to step outside your comfort zone and become what you want to be as a person, by becoming your own boss or working at a place of employment where you actually feel passion, looking forward to attending work every day? Become the "bird with the song." I dare you to live your passion that is not being lived.

Question yourself: What was I born to do? What is my life's purpose?

I ask you, what is your passion? What will make you sing out loud, becoming the bird with a song to sing? What do you love to do when the hours just fly? Pondering these types of questions will eventually lead you to your life's purpose.

I was a professional singer/songwriter. I spent thirty years singing in rock bands in both original and in cover bands. I absolutely loved it and gave all that I had to succeed—from working on my vocal abilities to bettering myself as a guitarist, creating and learning my professional home studio, and more. Band rehearsals would run for about three hours, sometimes four. However, I always gave rehearsal 100 percent, as if I were performing a show. The hours would just fly by, and as rehearsal would end, I always wanted to book more studio time instead of going home. Sometimes, we did rehearse a few more hours. It was amazing to me: I would always have the energy to give more, for the simple reason that music was my passion.

Passion creates the stamina and energy to keep you going. I couldn't imagine sitting in an office that long. I'd be looking at the clock every five minutes, struggling to stay awake, drifting into a *nana-nap* type of coma. Other people might love working in an office. For them, the hours fly by, and they will eagerly perform some overtime after an already busy day. Finding what you are good at and what you love—discovering your passion—is a blessing, leading you to a more fulling and happier lifestyle.

For me, my passion for working as a psychic medium holds the same energy as my music career once did. I really don't know about other psychic mediums, but if I'm beaten and tired, Spirit has shown me that I can still be successful at performing a reading.

One day, I was exhausted after working long hours within my business. I just wanted to go home and sleep. I finished work this rainy afternoon, so pleased that the day was over and I could go home to rest. I sat in my car for a few minutes to get my thoughts together before I travelled home, but little did I know that my spirit guides had other ideas.

I received a message to go to Strandbags to purchase my luggage for an upcoming trip to York Harbor, Maine, in the USA. I questioned my guides, asking, "Do I really have to go to Strandsbags?" The answer came through me as definite *yes*. As I again questioned my spirit guides, "Do I have to go now?" they instructed me to go to my regular coffee shop to see one of the owners, Raye.

Trust, trust, trust.

I showed up at the cafe as Raye was arriving. She greeted me and asked what she could do for me. "I don't know," I replied. "I was sent here."

"By who?" she asked inquisitively. I just smiled and pointed to the sky. She laughed as she knew very well what I meant and was no stranger to my spiritual ways.

Remembering my guide's instructions, I said to Raye, "You are well travelled?" I said, "I'm going to the States and need to buy luggage!"

Raye didn't blink an eye and said, "You have to get a security bag if you are travelling to the States, and you must go to Strandbags.

I was amazed as I realised that my guides had given me validation by sending me first to the cafe, where Raye told me to head over to Starndbags. Raye and I laughed. Then I said thank you and left to drive over to the next town, where the store was located.

I ended up at Stranbags, where I found that I had to do a reading for a lady. Spirit's timing was perfect. The message that I was to deliver was delivered at exactly the right time. I won't say too much about this, as I don't have permission. However, the person needed to hear the message that I was sent to convey to give her the strength to keep going forward. I was amazed! I am always surprised at the outcome of the readings I perform—particularly at times when I'm tired.

I had to experience the faith and trust it took to follow through, witnessing the healing I brought to someone. Only a few hours earlier, I was headed home for a well-deserved rest. This is a common occurrence with me. I have also coined the phrase "driveway readings" because of these unexpected happenings.

CHAPTER 2

LISTENING TO THE UNIVERSE

Practice the art of sitting in silence. Practice daily, or every other day, at the same time, and you will begin to hear the universe. Have you ever listened to the sound of silence?

—Doc O'Toole

An example of listening to the universe through signs and symbols:

Late in 2016, I receive a symbol of a "golden finch." Although I love birds and animals in general, I had never heard of the little bird called golden finch, although I knew that this was a significant sign sent to me. I wondered: What could this symbol possibly be referring to? At the time, I had been a student at a mediumship workshop here in Australia, and I decided to ask the teacher conducting the mediumship class if she had any thoughts on this, as I described the bird to her. It happens, that the teacher had lived in the USA for a time and stated that the bird I was referring to was called a golden finch, but she had no thoughts on what the message was about. Well, at least I had a lead. I had the name of the bird, and I knew the bird's native habitat.

I did many hours of research on this particular bird, but no answers resonated within me. Exhausting my research, I put the symbol of this beautiful-looking bird on my "metaphysical shelf," which is my imaginary shelf where I put signs, symbols, and messages that haven't fully matured.

Moving forward to 2018, I again attended the John Holland Advanced Mediumship Workshop in Maine. I usually arrive from Australia about four days before the workshop commences so that I can recover from jet lag and take in the sights. Every morning at 5:30 a.m., I would stroll along the beach and the scenic walkways of the Atlantic Ocean. I always feel right at home on the East Coast and dream of living in this part of the world as I stroll along, taking in the breathtaking scenic view. It's a feeling of "This is where I belong." It's that same intense feeling of *being home* I had when I first arrived in Boston the year before.

On the first morning walk, I was crossing a parking area as I headed up towards the track along the ocean clifftop when I saw a small toy dinosaur laying on the ground. I knew that this also was a sign put there on my path by the universe for me to recognise and take note of, while also placing the dinosaur on my "metaphysical shelf." I thought some little fellow had lost his favourite toy, so I left it there where it lay, hoping the person who had lost it would find it. For five days, I woke up for my morning walk, each day walking past the lost dinosaur lying there on the ground, just off of the edge of the grass area.

On that fifth day, a Saturday, after lunch, I went for a walk with my friend Jen to get some fresh air and to ground myself before class resumed for the afternoon. On our walk, I showed Jen the dinosaur and explained the circumstances. As we were walking along, talking and enjoying the afternoon sun, Jen directed me off of the pathway to a grassy park area. In the green park area, we stopped and chatted about the workshop and mediumship as we looked over the glistening ocean. I noticed how peaceful and serene the atmosphere had become. Suddenly, I heard a bird fluttering about, high above, in the tall tree in front of us.

I looked up, and to my surprise, it was a golden finch. *Oh, wow!* I was so excited. Being a native of Northern Carolina, Jen wondered what the fuss was all about. I explained that the golden finch had been a symbol for me, which had came to me a few years back, and that until now, I had forgotten all about it. I looked to the right to another smaller tree, where I noticed a bird's nest with a piece of paper sitting in it. I could just see the tip of the paper sticking up out of the top of the small nest. By this time, Jen thought I was nuts, but I was inquisitive and had to find out what was on the piece of paper. No stranger to the bushland, I was going up that tree to get that piece of paper, so off I went.

By this time, Jen likely had me suited up for a size XL straitjacket with double stitching and extra buckles. As I climb the tree to retrieve the piece of paper, I could not believe the image that was on it. Jen was quite curious now as I exclaimed, *"Oh, man! How cool is this!"*

"What? What?" Jen exclaimed. Jen would soon put my straitjacket back on the shelf and request a refund from the retailer as she now wanted to see for herself why I was so blown away by a piece of paper in a bird's nest.

Jen questioned me, "Well, what's on the piece of paper?"

I said, "You're not going to believe this. It's an image of a dinosaur." We stood there amazed, staring at the picture of the dinosaur. "How amazing is this," I exclaimed, "to find a symbol in a bird's nest?" It had all started with the golden finch symbol that came to me a few years earlier, which had been sitting on my "metaphysical shelf" all this time, collecting dust.

I read the sign as a message to leave the nest, to take my first real flight. It was time to now soar to new heights, to step out of my comfort zone, to take the next step towards my calling. This meant it was now time for me to take my mediumship up a level, to start performing platforms, also known as group readings. Although I had done group readings in the past, I mostly conducted one-on-one sittings. Following this surprising discovery, I said to Jen that I was going back to my room to get ready for the second half of the mediumship class.

Leading up to that Saturday afternoon, I began to get major static electric shocks, which is typical for me. The electric shocks seem to intensify at times when I'm to perform mediumship, or a message needs to come through from spirit. This, of course, could well be a coincidence, and I have no proof of this, only my observations. The static build-up is so intense within me that sometimes when I touch my digital alarm clock, I can get zapped, which results in my digital clock resetting itself.

Back in my room, I was getting large zaps, left, right and centre, from almost everything that I touched. This can be very annoying, but over the years, I have become used to it, mostly touching objects with the back of my hand when the static electricity in me is intensified, which can be for weeks on end.

Back in the workshop that evening, for the last module of the day, I was, to my surprise, the first person to be called up to perform a group reading. Laura, John Holland's assistant, handed me the mic as I stood up to walk to the stage area. With mic in hand, standing in front of the class, I gave a short introduction of myself, giving myself time to connect with Spirit. Without saying too much, I connected with a father figure very much straight away. I could see him standing there on a New York City street as I brought through the message for his loved one sitting in the audience. It was a fantastic connection, with the validation of a photo that was later texted to the recipient from her son, quite unexpectedly. I was blown away when the lady whom I had passed on the message to came up to me after class, showing me the photo that very much related to the message she had just received. It was incredible, to say the least.

There are many stories like this that I would like to share, possibly in another book, but what I also found incredible on that Saturday is that I had shared a table and a meal at lunchtime with both Daphne and Jen. Out of the whole class, the two ladies, along with myself, were called up by John Holland and Janet Nohavec to perform a group reading in front of the class. What are the odds of that? Oh yeah, and the toy dinosaur, on my Sunday morning walk, was not where it had laid lost on the ground for that past week, it was nowhere to be found. Hopefully, the little dinosaur made it back to its owner.

Have you ever stopped to wonder why you keep seeing the numbers 11:11, 222, 333, 444? Have you wondered why you started seeing feathers in random places where you usually wouldn't see a feather? One way you can begin to understand this is to listen to the universe in meditative silence, to ask your higher self, "What is the meaning of this repeating sign?"

Your higher self, or your spirit guides, is one way to begin learning to communicate with higher sources. You can ask Spirit, your angels, your spirit guides, or whomever you feel comfortable with, "Why do I keep seeing these types of numbers every time I am internally prompted to look at the time? Regularly seeing the number 11:11 is a pretty incredible thing to witness day after day when you feel prompted to look at the time—especially if you consider that the number 11:11 appears only twice within twenty-four hours.

A feeling of being *prompted* shows that you are listening to the internal voice of your body, that you have already begun to hear, although possibly without actually realising it. When you recognise this occurrence, know that it is all a matter of "one step at a time" as you begin to grow and listen to the internal senses that you were born with.

Asking for a sign. Asking for a sign from your divine source is relatively easy. Whether it is out loud or within your mind, all you have to do is ask. The first thing I'd suggest you do is to choose and recognise your personal symbols that resonate for you, like a lady beetle/bug, a type of bird, or even a feather—whatever connects you with something or with someone significant in your life. This type of practice will begin to align you with the workings of the universe, strengthening you and helping you to understand how you personally work. The more you practice, the sharper and more intuitive you will become. It's a good idea to start to become used to and to understand your own inner feelings. With time and patience, you will become proficient at recognising signs and symbols that are meant only for you—these signs and symbols are sent to you by the universe to help guide you throughout your life.

Not every feather or bird is a sign. As time goes by, you will begin to understand that feeling of "just knowing." Therefore, you will know instantly what your personal symbols are when they land on your pathway. I strongly recommend keeping up a daily awareness of what is around you, practising and fine-tuning your new found skill, documenting your findings in a journal along the way.

When I see one of my specific signs, such as a dragonfly, I smile knowingly and say, "Hello." Even if it is a message for me or just a random dragonfly out for a daily flight, I mostly know straight away what a symbol or sign is conveying to me, and I will often acknowledge the sign or symbol by asking quietly, "What are you trying to show me?" Don't sit around waiting for the answers, as the answer will be revealed to you in good time. You can ask any questions that you like. Be mindful, however, not to be overly detailed in your questioning, as it is not necessary.

Another classic technique, which I had heard of before and used myself, is when you are driving downtown, ask the "parking angels" for a parking spot. A common prayer that you may use is, "Parking angels, full of grace, please find me a parking space." It sounds funny and seems a little weird, but saying these words always puts a smile on my face, and I'm always amazed that this prayer usually works for me, as it does for a lot of other people as well. It goes to show, by putting your thoughts out there into the universe, you set the universal laws of energy into action, creating an outcome.

We are born as free spirits. This is respected throughout the universe. If you need help or guidance, you must ask Spirit, who is omnipresent, who is always there waiting to answer your call. Don't try to dictate how you want things to turn out. Be patient and watch the miracles unfold before you in the perfect way of divine timing.

For example, say the prayer, "Archangel Michael, I need your help with this situation." Then the situation, in divine timing, will be sorted out for you, most likely in unexpected ways. Sometimes, if you are to learn from what you are going through, nothing will be done, which you will appreciate more later in your life. In these types of scenarios, you will become much more grateful for that particular learning period. Always remember to keep the faith within you and within the divine energies.

> *Note:* Many years ago, I purchased Dennis Lynn's book *"Sign Posts"*. This is a great book to start you off fine-tuning your new awakened ability and understanding signs.

Angel numbers. If you continually see number sequences in your day-to-day life, know that this is a way for your angels to contact you or to simply tell you that they are with you, supporting you and that you are safe and never alone.

As mentioned earlier, you may begin to see 1111, 222, 333, or 444, which are the most common numbers you will start to witness as you begin your transition. You may continually wake at 3:33am, or 4:44am each morning of a new day. These number sequences may begin to appear perhaps when you are going through a challenging time when you need support and guidance. These numbers will bring you comfort once you start to understand the associated meanings. These meanings can be found via a Google search or in books. Doreen Virtue is one author I know of who has a book covering the meanings of numbers.

Since owning my ability as a psychic medium, I have become much more open to talking with friends and associates about signs, symbols, angels, and the spiritual energies that surround us. I have continuously shared with certain people in my life my understanding of angel numbers. These people have, in turn, become quite versed in the meanings of numbers, currently holding the answers within themselves when seeing the repeated numbers in their daily lives as they run their households or businesses. Coming to understand the meanings of numbers has repeatedly helped my friends through their lives, and they are now telling *me* what the numbers mean.

Liza Davidson is a close friend. Sometimes, while she is out on a road trip with her family, I will occasionally receive a phone call starting with something like, "Hey, Doc, I'm just calling to ask you a question. I keep seeing the number 555. It's been happening for weeks, and today, it's amplified. I see these numbers everywhere. What does this mean?"

To this, I will respond, "You already know what it means, Liza! What do you think it means?" After listening to Liza's interpretation of what 555 means to her, I will say, "See, you already knew the meaning of the numbers!" I will then complete the conversation with a little psychic input, adding the cherry on top of our discussion. It may sound a bit harsh, but I'm responding with questions to help build the faith within the person asking the questions, especially if I know that they already possess the answers they seek within them.

Conversations and songs. Have you ever had a problem for which you needed an answer? You may have found at times throughout your life that you needed an answer for a question that was bothering you. Since water is conductive, you may have found, without thinking about it, while taking a shower, that the answer to a problem automatically shows up within your thoughts. Other times, you may overhear a conversation while waiting in line at a checkout. The conversation usually has nothing to do with your question, but a keyword will trigger the answer that you needed to hear.

Another way of finding the answer to a question is to listen to a repetitive song in your thoughts. Likewise, each time you turn the radio on, you may uncannily hear the same song playing. When this happens, take note of the song title and lyrics, and feel what resonates with you. This may, for example, be a message from a passed loved one sending you a message of love, stating that they are okay and very happy where they are and not to worry about them. Or perhaps they simply need you to know that they are with you at that particular time. These are just a few examples, out of many, of how the universe converses with us and how you may communicate with the universe. Don't be in a hurry to learn if you are new to this way of understanding the world in a much brighter light. Take your time, and really feel what is yours and what is not for you within the messages that you receive.

I started listening to and seeing signs much more seriously way back in the early 1990s. This is not to say that I didn't consciously live by signs. More so, I began to respect them, listening to them as I became more in tune with the understandings of signs and symbols. Two years earlier, my psychic abilities started to increase. One particular day, I unconsciously began predicting that the phone was going to ring right down to the millisecond before it actually rang. I'd look randomly at the phone or think that the phone was going to ring, and a second later, to my surprise, I'd hear that familiar sound of the phone ringing.

At first, I found this a little odd and put it down to coincidence as I continued with what I was attending to at the time, seeing this happenstance a little amusing. What knocked that coincidental notion out of the park though was that one day, this scenario happened at least a half dozen times, which was very unusual. In those days, the phone did not ring as often as it does these days, with the convenience of mobile phones.

Unexpectedly, I would look at the phone, and it would ring. I remember the vision that I held in my mind at that time. I could see myself sitting on the fence, filled with scepticism. This mental vision showed me that I had been sitting on the fence for many years but as a healthy sceptic. Well, as you already have guessed, from that day forward, I began to slowly open up to the fact that I was a psychic. I began to slowly acknowledge my abilities and then push them aside. I was back and forth with this part of me for many years.

From that day forward, strange events started happening to me more and more often. I now needed to find the answers to begin to understand what was taking place with me. I would purchase books, looking for the knowledge, trying to understand and build on my psychic awareness which had been awakened deep within. Sometimes books would show up along my pathway, always at the exact time, I needed them. I studied up on subjects such as Native American culture and beliefs, which I am a massive fan of.

Edgar Cayce books began to show up after I watched a random old black-and-white movie on TV. The film was about Edgar Cayce; I think it was titled *The Sleeping Prophet*. The internet was relatively new at this time—well, really, what was the Internet? The World Wide Web was basically nonexistent in my world at that time. You had to learn the best way that you knew how, whether it be through books or likeminded people—who were rare to find as the Internet at that time here in Australia.

There was a strange knowing of what to do to practice and learn my abilities, to hone my craft living within me as if I had been doing this kind of work my whole life. As I remember, the knowledge seemed to be preprogrammed in me. As I began to work on and understand my abilities, I realised that situations and events that I believed everyone naturally knew about were starting to show me otherwise. I recognised that not everyone on this earth is in tune with their naturally gifted abilities with which they were born.

I remember the first thing that I realised, which was that I could see auras around plants, trees, bushes, and mountainous wooded areas. I'd seen this my whole life. So naturally, I thought that everybody could see them as well. This knowledge was to set me further on my awakening journey. I began to hear disembodied voices, with my name being called out while knowing that nobody else was in the room or building. However, this didn't stop me from checking to see if there was anybody in the room, in which case, there hadn't been.

Clairvoyant sight also started to take place as I predicted many times seeing events unfold while also helping friends with what I could see for them. The last time my visions were that strong had been in my late teens. Now, I had become stronger, seeing clairvoyantly much more vividly than before. Thinking back, I had pushed away my abilities and buried them deep within me, although they surfaced randomly many times throughout the years.

Supernatural things were happening in my apartment that I had been renting at the time. I lived by myself in a one-bedroom apartment in South Strathfield, Australia. At the time, I was working as a chief at Sydney airport in the domestic terminal staff canteen. One day, I arrived home after a busy day. While standing in my lounge room area, I went to check my answering service for messages, which was in an area out of the way of my typical day-to-day living area, over behind the lounge. To my surprise, I found that the power cord was totally unplugged. I very rarely had visitors—actually, not very often at all—so I was puzzled and amazed at what had happened. I put it down to higher energy trying to grab my attention.

One day, I ventured out and headed to Balmain for the day. Balmain is a suburb of Sydney. I have always liked the energetic feel of that particular area.

I had always been fascinated with mystics and spiritual subjects. However, at that time, I didn't know very much about it at all. I walked into a crystal shop on Darling Street, Balmain. I wandered around in the store in my own world, as I usually do, taking in all the products on display among the aroma of the incense-filled room. Not knowing why, I always felt comfortable in these types of stores, which felt a little like home. I spotted a variety of postcards portraying photographic images of Native Americans. I had been looking through these historical postcards, staring at them and feeling how it may have been way back then while trying to imagine their way of life. I had found it incredible that here I was, standing in a store, thinking of how the world had evolved and changed since the photos of these proud Native Americans were taken.

Take the lightbulb, for instance. The invention of the light bulb is credited to the inventor, Thomas Edison, coming from deep within the inventor's mind. I believe the idea came from the universe and downloaded to the inventor. In history, designs and ideas have come to their inventors through dream states or a solid knowing. Thomas Edison is well known for lucid dreaming and awakening with a new invention, sometimes finding the answers to complete a design already started. This is a classic example of listening to the universe, trusting in the universe and yourself, and having the faith to leap ahead to create inventions for the world to benefit from and to use in daily life situations, making life a little less arduous.

Walking out of the crystal shop in Balmain that sunny day set me on a new path of discovery. I didn't have much money at that time and very much lived day to day, living on the bread line. While standing outside the store, I felt this significant urge come over me, as if an invisible force had stopped me in my tracks. I felt a strong desire to go back into the store and purchase one of the postcards that attracted me. The card I had chosen was of Chief Joseph, chief of the Nez Perce tribe and leader of the Wallowa Band in the Pacific Northwest region of the United States. I paid for the postcard with the last few dollars I had. I was very proud to possess this historical card, and I headed back home, not really understanding what this was all about.

One night, I was in Smithfield, in Sydney's west, at a nightclub, supporting a friend's band, when another friend of mine at the time came up to me and said that he had a gift for me that he would give to me after the show. At the end of the night, my friend took me out to the parking lot where he had parked his car adjacent to the entry of the night club. He opened the boot of his car to reveal a large portrait, framed in wood and glass. It was a famous portrait of Chief Joseph. I was so excited and blown away at his generosity and the fact that Chief Joseph had made his presence known in my life once again.

A series of events of this nature happened again and again. Another night, while I was at home, I thought I would cook a pasta dish for dinner. Feeling like watching a movie, I rented a video from the shop downstairs from where I lived. I love Western movies and decided that that was the type of film that I would watch that night. The film was titled *I Will Fight No More Forever*, staring Ned Romero as Chief Joseph and Sam Elliot—one of my favourite actors—playing the part of Captain Wood. I never paid much attention to what the movie was about. I thought if Sam Elliot was in the movie, then it must be good.

I had the scene all set. Dinner was simmering away, and the Western movie was beginning. As the movie commenced, to my surprise, I realised that the film was a story on the life of Chief Joseph. I was stunned, to say the least.

As I was totally now focused on the beginning of this film, I noticed that the sizzling of the electric frypan behind me had dulled off—no more sizzling could be heard. As I went to check on my dinner, I saw that the electric frypan had been unplugged. Again I witnessed paranormal activity. I have never questioned why this happens to me. I have always felt comfortable and protected with these experiences and had an inner feeling, with a knowing of what it's all about.

I've had other electrical scenarios happen to me over the years, such exploding lightbulbs and continual static electricity in my body to this very day. I generally respond to myself by saying, *"How cool is that?"* Or, if I'm zapped, *"Ouch!"*

Most of the time, I have to touch metal objects with the back of my had before I can pick them up or grab hold, to make the shock less intense. I can be walking past a corner of a wall in my home and get zapped by the strip of metal that joins the corner of a gyprock wall.

A funny situation happened to me recently: I went to wash my coffee cup, which was cold and still half full of coffee. As I was walking over to the kitchen sink, ready to pour my coffee down the drain, my hand touched the edge of the metal sink. A powerful blue flash zapped as my hand touched the side of the sink, causing me to react strongly. In one quick-swoop reaction, I pulled my hand away from the sink, causing me to fling the coffee out of my mug, which landed all over the kitchen window, the bench, and the window sill—some actually made it to the sink. I just stood there and laughed my butt off, as did the onlookers. It reminded me of what an abstract artist might do to create a famous art piece, such as the renowned artist Pro Heart, an Australian-artist born in Broken Hill NSW.

I have been told by psychic readers over the years that I had been a medicine man in a past life. I've never really believed that to be true. However, at the same time, I'm very fascinated with Native American culture and have the highest respect for the Native Americans. I feel there is some kind of connection there, but I haven't delved into it yet.

I once performed a reading for a lady whose ancestors were from the Native American Shoshone tribe. I explained that I could see that there was someone quite famous for her ancestral heritage. She replied that it was Sacajawea, a guide for the Lewis and Clark expedition in the early 1800s. I don't remember many of the readings that I've performed over the years as the messages came through me, not from me. But when something significant comes from a reading such as this, I do remember the headline or some key points of the reading. I was over the moon with this historic result. I had always admired Sacajawea for what she had achieved at a very young age. I proudly carry an American coin in my medicine bag that depicts Sacajawea's image on one side.

Since Chief Joseph entered my life back in 1994, I have learned a lot about Native American culture and their tribal beliefs. This is all from listening to the universal whispers and trusting to spend my last dollars on a Native American postcard instead of buying something to eat. I have since worn a medicine bag and still do to this very day.

Being aware of numbers, signs, and symbols will help you throughout your life. I'm so glad that I received the numbers 333 as I was writing this chapter, which seems to be writing itself. The number 333 is a sign that your angels are around you ready to assist you, which also indicates you're on the right path and on track.

While living in Burradoo, a suburb of Bowral in the Southern Highlands, I began to experience a lot of small miracles, which I like to call *serendipities*. These small miracles were absolutely fantastic. My psychic and mediumistic abilities were becoming stronger every day. As mentioned in a previous chapter, I finally began to step into my life's purpose, listening more intently than ever before to the universe, Spirit, and my guides.

My guides, by the way, are known as "Sun Bear and Crew." This name came to me through a reading that I had at a Mind, Body, and Spirit Festival. Two weeks after the festival, not actually believing in what I was told, I decided—or more to the point had a feeling—to perform a spirit guide meditation. I saw a very clear image in black and white of a Native American called Sun Bear. I did an image search on Google and found the image that I had seen in my spirit guide meditation. That's when I believed in who my spirit guide was. So maybe the previous readings that I'd had received over the past twenty years or so now hold an essence of truth.

In 2013. I had taken up the reins to my abilities, making a solid decision to dedicate my life to helping people with my gifts and abilities as a psychic medium. Since that time, I've performed hundreds of readings, witnessing transformations and healings in people's lives. I'm so honoured to be apart of those lives, while at the same time honouring and cherishing my abilities with the utmost respect.

I often wonder what I would be doing and where I would be now if I had fully understood and listened to Spirit over twenty years ago, the possibilities are endless. I didn't see or understand that I could be working in this metaphorical field. Working in this type of industry requires a deep understanding and caring of people, as I can now shed some light on people's lives while helping my clients through difficult times, which I find very rewarding and gratifying indeed.

At the time, all those years ago, when my abilities came on strong, my singing career had been most important to me. The skills that I had honed and crafted as a frontman, singing in the many bands that I was a part of, now are applied in different fields, such as public speaking, which I now look forward to becoming more involved with. Looking ahead, I intend to be involved in more presentations and public speaking at seminars, sharing my knowledge to further help people understand themselves through my gathered knowledge and understandings. Though there are many already out there sharing their knowledge, some well-known, some not so famous. I believe that it is our responsibility to pay forward our knowledge for others to gain some insight for themselves. After all, isn't this what we are all supposed to be doing, helping mankind with our skills and abilities, no matter how great or small our abilities are? One kind gesture, helping hand, a listening ear, or a kind word is really all it takes to make a difference in this world while providing constant reminders that we are all students of the universe.

Listening to the universe is an ability that we all have within us, something we are all born with. Listening to the universe involves listening to your body, feeling your feelings, understanding your knowing, and listening to your inner subjective voice.

Here is a classic everyday example of feeling and listening to your inner self that occurs when you are sitting with a group, engaging in conversation:

You are trying to speak, to be involved, wanting to inject your point of view. You find that each time you go to talk, you are cut off, and no one seems to hear from you. Finally, on the third or fourth try, you speak a little louder, communicating what you wish to say. But as you are expressing your piece, you realise how irrelevant your comment may be, as you begin to plummet like a spitfire in World War Two. Your friends seem to politely ignore your comment, giving you a parachute to land safely. It's always a good idea to sit in silence and listen objectively as the stories unfold before you.

When this happens, ask yourself: Who or what is trying to stop you from speaking of that which you perceived to be relevant? Your spirit guide or guides could be the answer here. I've tested it out a few times just to experiment while taking mental notes of the results that transpired. What I found is a feeling of an invisible magnetic pull trying to stop me from conversing. When you stop and think about it, your comment may hold no bearing on the topic of conversation at all. You just want to be apart of the conversation. Other times, you could be in a conversation, speaking a complete paragraph while finding that no one has actually heard you speak at all. It's a bit like those old silent movies.

Have you ever walked into a room within your home or office and felt that a chair placed under the window didn't feel right in its current position? You then decide to move the chair to a corner, where it *feels* now to be in its rightful place of display. What you are doing here is listening to your body while taking note of how your body feels with the chair now in another position of the room rather than the previous position, under the window.

Close friends of mine have a young teenage son named Hugh. He is a classic young man and into anything and everything. Hugh was about thirteen years old at the time when he rang me in a panic. He is very aware of my abilities, and on this particular day, he needed my help. I answered, "Hey, Hugh, what's happening."

He replied, "Doc, you've got to help me. I know you can help me."

Hugh was in a panic, so I slowed him down and asked what the problem was while trying to stay calm and relaxed myself, thinking the worst had happened.

Hugh explained in a panicked voice, "Doc I was out riding along the bike track and lost my new iPhone. It fell out of my pocket."

I slowed him down again, speaking to him very calmly. "Hugh, tell me exactly where you are, and stay outside the bike track so I can see you. I'm on my way. Just breathe deeply and slow your roll. Everything will be okay."

Hugh had purchased his new iPhone with borrowed money from his mum. To his credit, he was working after school to pay his mother back the money that he had borrowed. After sitting in my car and asking for divine help from archangel Michael, I drove off to meet young Hugh at the bike track, where he had been zooming around, having a fun time on his bicycle. It was just on dusk, and the bike track was in a bushland area, making it difficult to find his treasured new iPhone, which might've been anywhere in long grass or amongst the bushland areas. As expected, Hugh had been flying over jumps and doing wheel stands and all kinds of activities on his bicycle that a young fellow would be doing, all without a care in the world.

Poor Hugh—when I got to him, he was so distraught. I met up with his mother, Liza, on the way to meet Hugh. As I walked up to him, it was obvious how upset he was. I slowed him down to recount his steps and movements along his ride. Hugh can get a little flighty at times—he cracks me up—so slowing him down took a little while, but I eventually, got him back on track.

Suddenly, I saw a huge white feather. I called out to Hugh and asked him what the feather meant. He was reluctant to say, so I encouraged him to speak his thoughts. Eventually, he said, "It's a sign."

"Yes," I replied. "A sign of what?" I asked him.

Hugh replied, "Angels?"

"That's right," I said. I explained that all we had to do now was look for the signs that would lead us to the iPhone.

A little while after, not even five or ten minutes, Hugh was calling out, "Doc, Doc, here's another feather … and another."

I was amazed, as feathers were leading a trail towards his lost iPhone. I continued to encourage him, saying, "Keep on believing. We're getting closer."

I asked Hugh's mother to start ringing Hugh's phone constantly to light up the screen, as night began to fall upon us. Hugh was now full of positivity and riding ahead of us on his bicycle, of course, with a few wheel stands thrown in for good measure.

All of a sudden, he yelled out again, enthusiastically, "Doc, here is another white feather!" And again he yelled, "Doc, Doc, and here is my iPhone!" he yelled at the top of his voice. There was his iPhone, with the screen lighting up the now dark atmosphere. Wow! I too was amazed.

Hugh was so happy and very grateful seeing that final white feather as Hugh's mother rang his phone, illuminating the screen so that Hugh could find it in the dark among the bushes off to the side of the track. He was totally over the moon, not to mention relieved.

We began walking back as Liza's husband, Rod, arrived on the scene. Everyone was so excited and sharing stories as we ventured off back to Hugh's home. He was so grateful. We all left there with new experiences and the lessons of listening to the universal energies while keeping out a keen eye for the signs and symbols. I was amazed at this Sunday-evening adventure with Spirit. More so, I was happy about the experience that a young thirteen-year-old Hugh had witnessed it firsthand, an experience that he will now carry throughout his lifetime.

Eight months after Hugh's lost phone experience, he told me a story. He and his buddies got lost while bushwalking. They weren't sure which track they were to take on their way back home, so he took control of the situation and led his friends out to safety. Hugh explained that they didn't know which way to go when suddenly, he saw a white feather. He repeated what he had learned from his situation many months before, with the lost iPhone incident. Hugh had followed a trail of feathers, which he now understood to be a divine sign, knowing help is never too far away. He had followed the track of feathers, leading himself and his friends out to safety onto the right trail home. Shortly after, he and his friends arrived home safe and sound with another great adventure story to share.

What a fantastic experience, to witness and receive divine spiritual help, especially at Hugh's young age, but also trusting in himself and the universal energies. Hugh now listens to the universe, keeping faith in the divine energies around him. He is so inquisitive about spiritual happenings that I find it amazing. Hugh is like a duck to water when it comes metaphysics or anything for that matter. He also is a deep thinker and usually has a question or two to ask me when I visit.

As the story of Hugh demonstrates, listening and watching for signs and symbols and being in tune with yourself and the universe, having faith in oneself, can be of great benefit to you throughout your lifetime. All you have to do is to let go and have faith.

CHAPTER 3

BE KIND TO YOURSELF AND OTHERS

I challenge you to start being kind to yourself. By doing this, you will be able to be entirely of service to others.

—Doc O'Toole

We all desire and strive to lead a happier lifestyle. Start by administering kindness to yourself and others. With this outlook on life, you will begin to witness that positive energies and happiness are beginning to transform you internally. There is no secret to being kind to you; all you have to do is to start.

It doesn't take months to learn how to administer kindness to yourself. I challenge you over the next thirty days to start living a life of prosperity. Do this by enjoying your life, giving yourself permission to live a more positive lifestyle, with a feeling of worthiness. We are all worthy, no matter what your background may be. Begin your transformation today by turning on the key of happiness, steering yourself all the way to success. You will then begin to ride along your new highway of freedom to a much happier, more fulfilled lifestyle.

You may not believe that you are worthy of happiness. On the contrary, thinking you are here merely to be of service to others is an incomplete understanding of your life's purpose.

We are all created equal. With this in mind, it says that we are all deserving of living a joyfully fulfilled life. So you may as well get on board with your God-given talents and make the best of what you possess with your specific skills, that you inherited at birth. Do this while living your life to the fullest, daring to be you, by stepping right outside of your comfort zone. This is when we truly begin to live.

At times, it may seem that we are living in a mundane way, questioning yourself: Why me? Why does this always happen to me? When will my turn for happiness ever arrive? This is only what we perceive to be true. In fact, if you step outside of the "poor me" syndrome, you will clearly see that it is your personal responsibility to make it happen, that we are witnessing our own individual personal growth as we learn life lessons, therefore always putting into practice our "striving to be better routine".

We can then use our newly learned knowledge and understandings to help others in this world, who are struggling with similar issues that we also have struggled with. Take these lessons and embrace the teachings to then pass on your learned experience to others in need. By doing so, we evolve to a new, higher level, helping others in the process, keeping in mind that we are all equal.

It is an absolute honour to be apart of this ever-evolving world. Sharing, learning, and helping others is precisely what we are doing here. It is an honour to be a part of life in this way. We are all a part of the bigger picture, as we all have a role to play in the canvas of life. It may take you half a lifetime to get on board, and that is okay. However, we eventually must venture out into the world, out into our community, helping those in need—learning, evolving, while becoming a better you.

One example of happiness is to see and understand that you have been restraining who you genuinely are, blocking what you truly deserve. Remember that love takes care of its own. Have a really good look in the mirror and see yourself the way those close to you, such as your loved ones, really see you. Don't be too hard on yourself; I guarantee that it's a better picture than you paint yourself to be.

While staring at your reflection in the mirror, someone will be staring back at you who is worthy, who does deserve self-respect. Take a few seconds out of your life, beginning now, by changing your mindset and releasing yourself from the restraints set by your own thought patterns. See life for what it truly is and what it can be, unguided by the negative noise you hear in your thoughts. When you decide to participate in the game of life instead of sitting on the sideline as a spectator, you will soon see what the world truly has to offer you, and more importantly, what you have to offer the world.

I was speaking with a client recently who was unhappily married. Don't get me wrong, I'd prefer to save a marriage, and I'm proud to say that I have done in the past, but if it's not working for some reason, then it's not working. She told me that she had to stay in her marriage for financial reasons. I replied, a little shocked, "Oh, really!" I then explained that that's not a reason. She said he had her by the balls. My reply was straightforward. "No, he doesn't. You don't have any," I exclaimed.

I continued to show her that she, too, could be financially independent and able to support herself if she so chose to. I said to Carol (not her real name), "Don't you have a yoga class that you run?"

She replied, "Yes, I run it out of a gym." I asked her how many students she had. Carol replied, "It depends on how many show up."

I looked at Carol strangely, a little perplexed by her statement. "What do you mean?" I asked. Well, as it turns out, Carol's yoga classes are not very well structured. Her classes are based on the vibe of "whoever feels like showing up will show up."

Skipping the details of why she runs her classes this way, I suggested that she get busy about getting serious, that she becomes more seriously business-minded, focusing on building her yoga class with a solid, more structured foundation. I explained that she could start promoting and building her client base. She could do this through word of mouth, creating an online platform, designing business cards, creating a website, and possibly renting a specific space for the purpose of her classes.

I suggested that she approach new-age stores to see if they had or knew of a place where she might be able to rent space to conduct her yoga classes on a more professional level. "Oh, and by the way, Carol," I said, "leave some business cards and flyers at the new-age stores that you visit." I also suggested that she create sidelines in the same field as her yoga classes. Then she could start to write a book on the subject or even develop seminars and workshops, teaching others the art of yoga in other ways as well as the traditional way.

That day, I believe that I made a dent in Carol's life. It took a while, but I think I made some progress towards helping her to understand and to see her capabilities. That is, moving out of the passenger's seat for the first time in a long while and, instead, taking control of the steering wheel, which takes faith, courage, and trust, while taking on a new belief and understanding in oneself.

Carol saw herself as defeated, living a fear-based lifestyle rather than living in the love energy, for which we all possess and strive for as we mature and grow towards the understanding of why we are here. It is important to understand energy and to harness the knowledge of how positive and negative energies truly work. Furthermore, I explained to Carol how important it is to have the knowledge and understanding of the spiritual energy that lives within each and every one of us in our day-to-day existence. This is where we should be living, to a much greater degree than we actually do.

The way that I see it, the world that we live in operates in two words: love and fear. Love attracts love, and fear attracts fear. Just stop and feel love for a minute or two. It feels fantastic, doesn't it? While love inserts an incredible energy feeling, it is a feeling of total freedom and bliss. On the contrary, fear feels quite the opposite, draining your energy, depleting your self-belief and self-confidence, leaving you with a negative mindset that can be self-sabotaging.

Love is the kryptonite against fear. We all are susceptible to the fear energy. However, with the knowledge of love as your kryptonite, you can combat the fear energy in a more prosperous, more understanding, and more knowledgeable way.

When someone is feeling defeated or negative, I have to do something about it. I can't help myself. It's a built-in trigger that I have learned to evolve with. Negativity is a big nay-nay in my books. It is also banned from my home. I will push a Mr Yeah-But or a Mrs Yeah-But, through the mists of self-sabotage or that of a negative mindset, clear into the blue clouds of positivity, happiness, and joy. I will show them that they are worthy, that they have just as much right as anyone else in this world to live in happiness and joy. I will highly encourage anyone who doesn't see their gifts, skill, and abilities to the point that they start to see the light that glows within them. They are usually just a step away from throwing off their self-imposed shackles, often placed there by themselves or by life's situations.

Carol's happy-go-lucky yoga students are naturally attracted by the energy that Carol puts out into the world. She, therefore, attracts students with the same mindset, who show up for a spot of yoga when they feel like it, without any real desire to take the art of yoga seriously. You've heard the old saying "like attracts like"? It's not just a saying; it is a fact. It's the *law of attraction*.

By the time Carol's session was completed, I could see a glint of positivity and possibilities of a brighter future in her eyes, more so than when she first walked in for her session. I know if she has a real go at creating her business, no matter what the subject of that business is, she will become financially independent. After this realisation, the sky, as they say, is the limit.

In time, Carol will witness her positive results, one step at a time, by stepping outside her comfort zone. Nothing will stop her from enjoying life to the fullest, transforming herself into an independently happy person. Who knows? This self-fulfilment may even save her marriage.

As always, I wish my clients all the best. I'm thrilled when they leave their session in a much happier and healthy thought space, rather than the uncertainty with which they may have entered at the beginning of their session. That means that I've done my job.

Go out in life and start kicking some field goals. You will be shocked at how capable you really are. Before you know it, you will be the captain of your own team. You will have jumped out of the passenger seat and into the driver's seat, navigating, steering towards your very own destination, your own destiny. Wow! What a way to live!

Stop for a minute, relax, and take a deep breath. Sit in a comfortable chair in loose-fitting clothing. Place your feet flat on the ground, with your hands resting on your lap. Now, breathe in through your nose, hold for four seconds, and then exhale for four seconds. Repeat this a few times. Now imagine how free and liberated you feel once you have set yourself on the new highway of life. A much better road, one without too many potholes, with a much smoother life journey and much better scenery. You now discover, *Wow, yes, it is possible. Yes, I do have what it takes.*

While in the meditative state of deep breathing and relaxation, imagine that you are looking at yourself in the mirror. You now see in the reflection of the mirror—you looking back at you.

Feel that, yes, you do have the power and strength. Yes, it is *you* looking back at you in your mirror. That's the person capable of all things and much, much more. This is all contained within you, although it is your job to bring it to the foreground.

Self-recognition is something we rarely give ourselves. Yet, we are quick to give others recognition for their own achievements. We should take pride in what we achieve, as it also inspires others.

It's a great thing to help others and acknowledge their personal achievements, by praising them for their skills as they kick their goals. Giving others encouragement is a kind and selfless act. However, there is also a fine line. You must also provide yourself with acknowledgment, accepting praise graciously when it is indeed bestowed upon you.

We, as humans always seem to push praise away from ourselves. I know, I used to. That is until I realised I had been creating blockages within myself by failing to acknowledge recognition. Energetically, you are telling the universe that you don't truly matter.

On the contrary, acceptance of praise speaks to the universe, expressing your gratitude for your skills, gifts, abilities, and birthrights. This creates a flow of positive energy rather than causing blockages, allowing unconditional acceptance from the one expressing praise for a job well done. Remember, we are all one and equal in the eyes of God (or whichever creator you believe in).

By refusing to accept praise and recognition, you are, in fact, self-sabotaging and pushing your abilities away. Never give your energy away to lift someone else up for the achievements that you have earned. Also, never put someone up on a pedestal. (Brass statues are excluded.)

You've earned the right to be praised; you own and retain the right and the gift of praise bestowed upon you.

You don't refuse a birthday gift that a friend has given you. A friend has gone out, spending their time, their thoughts, and their energies to get you something special, to provide you with something nice on your specific day. You were born at a particular time of the year, known as your birthday. Gratefully celebrate it; it is a blessing.

Celebrate, validate, and commemorate by owning your right to happiness. Acknowledge who you are. Acknowledge the gifts and abilities you have. We all, each and every one of us, are born with a specific gift and purpose for this lifetime, which begins here on earth on that very day that we are born. This day happens to be your memorial day.

On the contrary, appreciate and show gratitude for what someone has done for you. Unconditionally thanking a person for all that they do is in itself so gratifying.

On more than one occasion throughout my life, I have driven into a fuel station where there was a person who had not had the money with them to pay for the fuel they had put into their vehicle. The most recent time that I can remember was over a year ago, in my hometown. It was a busy Friday afternoon at the end of summer in 2016. That time of the afternoon, also being a Friday, it requires a little more patience to navigate through town in the chaotic, rushing traffic. People are tired from the week that they have worked. Mothers are scurrying their children around, picking them up from school, then taking them to music classes or sports training or picking up the groceries for the weekend. All the while, they just want to get home for "me time" to relax before the next wave of chores. You get the picture, I'm sure!

I fueled up my Ford ute, then proceeded towards the store to pay. There was a lineup of two lanes. I happen to be standing behind a nurse who had fuelled up her SUV. The problem was that Jenny (not her real name) had no money to pay for her fuel. In her rush that afternoon, she had forgotten to take her credit card with her. So, the poor lady was letting the cashier know of her predicament while asking if he could hold her driver's license until she could arrive back to pay her outstanding account.

I couldn't believe the cashier. He just stood there and repeated, with a blank look on his face, seemingly without a care, "You have to pay for the fuel."

I noticed that Jenny was wearing a nurse's uniform, which indicated to me that she is lightworker who enjoys helping others with their needs and nursing patients back to good health. I looked around at the other people waiting in line, which by this stage had become longer, stretching nearly out the door. I felt for this lady. I said to the cashier, "I will cover the cost of the lady's fuel." Jenny was amazed that I had offered to help her, and she thanked me with a relieved and grateful look on her face. I could see her stress level drop, and the colour in her face returned to normal.

Still, the cashier was wearing that same blank face, while not looking or showing a hint of acknowledgment or gratitude as he took *my* credit card and processed the transaction. I doubt very much if he even realised if I was male or female. The level of care was below zero. This didn't bother me, though, but it amazed me just the same.

Again, Jenny thanked me. She was so appreciative. I assured her that it was totally okay and that I was glad that I could be of assistance. After all, isn't that why we are here on this earth: to evolve, learn, and help our fellow man?

Jenny followed me out to my Ford ute, where she thanked me again before she drove off to take her young son, Steve, to his first-ever job interview. Before she left, Jenny insisted that I give her my details so that she could repay me. Not that it really mattered to me, but I accepted. We exchanged details, and a week later, she rang me while I was at work to thank me again and also to let me know that she had made a deposit into my bank account.

The Six Positive Outcomes

1. There was a lady in need of help. I chose to help her. It's the best feeling in the world to be of service, to be able to help someone in need. We all need a little help every now and then. It surely makes life that little bit easier. The energy and vitality that you feel from a simple act of kindness, lending a hand to another, is so invigorating. For example. If you are having a bad day and you help a complete stranger out by changing a tire on their car, your day automatically just got better. Don't you also feel this way when you offer a lending hand? I'm sure you do! The feeling is mutually fantastic, right? And the recipient also feels this way, as Jenny obviously felt.

2. Jenny graciously accepted help. Accepting help from another creates a positive flow of energy. Also, accepting from another is also doing them a favour. They want to help you, and when you do not wish to receive their help, they feel dissatisfied and a little annoyed. It sounds strange, but if someone offers you support, it's because they really want to help.

On the other hand, you may not want their help because you feel that you are bothering them or something of this nature. Not at all. Really think about this.

Has there ever been a good samaritan whom you have denied their right to give you kindness, who then looked a bit perturbed? That's because you have just robbed them of their free will to offer you a helping hand. Don't we always say, "No, no, I can do it" or "It's my problem? I can sort it out"? It all works in a perpetual circle—in reality, we are all giving. It just takes a participant to do the receiving to complete the circle.

Isn't it a lot better to move house with a group of friends willing to help you rather than moving house by yourself?

It took me about thirty moves to realise this. Thank God I learned my lesson! It would have been absolutely fantastic if I had learned this lesson about twenty-five moves ago.

3. I unconditionally gave Jenny help. This is very much self-explanatory—helping somebody unconditionally is helping straight from the heart because you care, because you want to help someone. No more, no less.

4. I accepted Jenny's thank-you. This is another thing we as humans are always guilty of: not accepting a helping hand. Help can be a tough thing to accept, or it can be easy. Complete the circle of giving by accepting!

Our pride (otherwise known as ego) sometimes gets in the way. Not accepting help also results from not believing that you are actually worthy. This could stem from your upbringing or certain beliefs that you may have learned along the way. I've said it before: it's a choice to be happy. It really is!

Changing how you think can begin right now, in the next second, through a thought. You have to work at the new you, but it is very possible to start seeing yourself in a positive new light, right now, this very moment. It's a choice!

Wallpaper of Affirmations

Many years ago, I once lived in a flat in Sydney above a shop. There was one wall that I wallpapered with affirmations, written on A4 paper. I would stand in front of the wall and read what I had written. By creating my wallpaper of affirmations, I sent a message to the universe reinforcing my words. It got to the point where friends would come over just to read the wall. An old friend of mine, Tyrone, used to do just that. I remember one night, Tyrone came over for a visit, and I made him a coffee as he ventured over to the wall of affirmations. Ty used to just stand there, with a coffee in his hand, and read my wall. He would jokingly say, "Doc, I only come over to read your wall." That was fine by me. "Read it to your heart's content," I would say.

5. I accepted Jenny's desire to return the money when she could. People look at money as the root of all evil—Yeah, right! Money is made up of a group of molecules, with ink and artwork on it. Because it has "five dollars" written on it, it enables you to purchase a coffee at your favourite local cafe. If those same group of molecules with ink and artwork displayed on it depicted the image of an eight of wands, this would indicate a tarot card with a mechanical meaning, possibly, "air travel, rapid communication, energy or progress." However, money, made up of molecules, is also energy. The more you deny the energy, the more you won't have the energy that you rightly deserve while attracting the opposite energies. So keep the energy flowing in your life in a positive direction, simply by accepting it. This sends a positive message to let the universe know, "Yes, I like it, which will inevitably attract more."

6. Jenny's stress levels lowered, and her son made it to his job interview. This is very cool! I look at this story as an example of the "butterfly effect." After reading the above account of helping a stranded lady, I realised that what transpired between Jenny and me had caused a ripple effect. Her son, Steve, was waiting to go to his first job interview at the Scottish restaurant, also known as the Golden Arches.

I can only imagine the conversation between the mother, her son—and her husband, for that matter—about what had transpired that day. She had filled her car with fuel and had no funds to pay for it. Jenny's son will grow up with this story firmly planted in his mind. Without a doubt, he will also pay it forward, all because of this story that transpired that day, when his mother had no money to purchase her fuel.

Steve too will be out in the world one day minding his own business, going about his day, and then come across a situation like an example written above. He will, without a doubt lend his own hand to a stranger in need, remembering the story of that day when someone helped his mother while she was stranded at a petrol station, many years before. This one good deed will have a ripple effect on the pond of life, bringing us one step closer to world peace.

The above six points became a reality of happiness and good feeling, for both Jenny and me, and of course, her family. It doesn't take much effort to be kind to someone. The internal rewards, one of feeling fantastic, create a positive, energetic ripple effect. It actually takes more energy to act negatively than it does to act positively, out of love. Creating positive energy actually creates even more positive energy within your life. The universal energies notice what you are attracted to, therefore dictating that if you like this type of energy, the universe will accommodate you with more of the same energy.

Perhaps you have read, or heard of, the book *The Law of Attraction*, by Esther and Jerry Hicks. There are also numerous other titles written about the subject of the law of attraction. There are hundreds of positive quotes, written by a whole lot of authors, all aimed at giving you positive affirmations to live by and to transform your life into a much better, vibrant and happy day-to-day living, with a bright and cheerful future illuminated ahead of you. One example of this type of affirmation that you can use for your own comes from Bob Proctor and Greg S. Reid's book, *Thoughts Are Things.* "If you see it in your mind, you will hold it in your hand."

I highly recommend applying these words and many others in your daily life. The magic begins to happen when you choose to be kind to yourself and others in this world, beginning at that very moment when you choose to have a positive mindset. It takes only one second to change the way that you think and feel. The magic that happens from that conscious choice is much more of a freedom lifestyle. It's a certain kind of magic.

CHAPTER 4

THE LIGHTWORKER

*I have seen people deploy a negative attitude towards others who dare to dream big to achieve great things in their lifetime. Contrary to this old belief, know that **"dreams are the blueprints to your future"**; in turn, this will lead you to your divine life's purpose.*

—Doc O'Toole

Who Are the Lightworkers?

Lightworkers are individuals who have agreed to incarnate upon this earth. They have a pre-agreed life's purpose of raising the consciousness of mankind to enlightenment. One of their main focuses is to expand light and love and to shine goodness into the hearts of humanity while living a life of servitude in a variety of ways. Mainly, lightworkers dedicate their lives of service throughout their existence here on this earth while spreading their goodwill selflessly. Some organisations, such as the Salvation Army and the Smith Family, work tirelessly at helping within their communities. Charity events, volunteer work, and organised nonprofit groups also band together to help the underprivileged and grief-stricken families, creating a less burdensome experience for the needy.

It would be nice to remember what our life goals were after we have incarnated, but mostly this is not so. That doesn't mean that it's wrong. Nor is it right. That's the way that it is intended to be. It's always better to not know the outcome of our purpose. Progressing through life in this manner will ultimately make us stronger as we learn and grow within ourselves.

Some lightworkers may live a harmonious lifestyle, while others may not experience such a fortunate time for many years. However balanced or unbalanced a human may or may not be within their lives up to the point of their enlightenment, they always seem to be in the right place at the right time, to be of assistance to those who have become lost along their journey.

Lightworkers commonly help mankind selflessly and without thinking. They can also be dealing with their own personal battles at the same time. The journey to owning and living up to your pre-incarnated agreement, to roam this world as an incarnated lightworker, has a growing period. I like to call it the "apprenticeship period." This would explain why it takes a half a lifetime to realise that your life's purpose is to serve and help others in a balanced and harmonious way, in a variety of fields, while living as a soul here on earth, experiencing and living a human existence. Lightworkers also have a pre-built-in ability of "just knowing" or "clear knowing." This is also known as claircognisance.

There are four significant *clair* senses. The following is a brief explanation of these senses.

- **Claircognizance** is one of the four major *clair* senses. This clair is the ability to "just know" the information that comes to you spontaneously. You know without a doubt that the information that you are receiving is totally, 100 percent accurate, without prior knowledge, and non-conversant; the information appears within your mind without any way to back up the acquired knowledge.
- **Clairvoyance** is having the ability to see clearly, seeing images like flashcards in your mind. Also, you may see a video scene playing out within your mind, as I mostly do.

- **Clairsentience** is the ability to receive intuitive messages through feelings, emotions or the feeling of physical sensations.
- **Clairaudience** is the ability to clearly hear those in spirit, speaking to you either internally through your mind (which is hearing objectively) or externally, (hearing objectively) sometimes referred to as a disembodied voice. One example of hearing a disembodied voice is to listen to your name being called out when there is clearly no other person around.

I remember when I first heard a disembodied voice calling out my name. It was 1995. I was managing a factory in the Sydney suburb of St. Peters. It was a sunny summer afternoon as I attended to work at the factory. The factory had been unusually quiet that mid-afternoon, as all the delivery drivers were out on their rounds, making deliveries to the awaiting mechanical shops.

While I was focused on the job at hand that sunny afternoon, a voice appeared out of nowhere. The sound of this voice was clearly audible. As clear as crystal, I heard my name being called out. Even though I knew that I was by myself, I still looked around behind me to see no one standing there at all, which I sort of knew would be the case. However, at the same time, I somehow knew that the voice I had just heard was a divine voice. I got up from where I had been working at the time and walked around the factory to see if anyone else had arrived without my knowledge. As I looked around, I could see no one in sight, which I instinctively thought would be the end result.

Hearing this disembodied voice did not frighten me at all, although I was very surprised. Instead, I thought it was really cool. It actually put a smile on my face, completing my day. I naturally accepted my experience and continued my work enveloped by a feeling of comfort.

Although I had embraced this experience, I never spoke of this day for many years. To me, it didn't seem relevant to any conversation. It was an experience that I held dearly within. That day had been a divine blessing. It was something special that I had experienced, a cherished moment in my life. The next time I heard a disembodied voice would be many years later, in March 2010. This time, I was very surprised, as I had been travelling along a freeway, deep in my own thoughts. As I drove, my thought process was interrupted by a voice coming from the passenger side. This time, it delivered me a message that had been an answer to my thoughts. However, again, this didn't bother or shock me. Like many years before, I didn't feel afraid, just surprised and elated about the return of the spiritual voice.

It was three years after the third time that I had witnessed a disembodied voice, in 2013, when my spiritual awareness opened up quite strongly within me—much stronger than the previous years had been. In full flight, this marked the beginning of dedicating my life to being of service to mankind, by working as a psychic medium.

It had taken me many years to answer my spiritual calling. Now being of service with my gifts and abilities, and also sharing the knowledge that I had accumulated over the years, I knew without a doubt that my true purpose and calling had now begun. Finally, my life's purpose had arrived. Not that I knew what my life's purpose was up to that point. However, I definitely knew and acknowledge what I was to do when that day arrived. This is the time when I adopted a deep knowing, which I would dedicate the rest of my life, using my abilities, for the sole purpose of helping mankind, therefore stepping up to answer my calling. I can just hear my guides as they wipe the sweat from their brow, with a deep sigh of relief, saying, "Finally! He now gets it."

As a psychic medium, reading for my clients on a one-on-one basis, I found that counselling also comes into play, further helping my clients. You really can't counsel anyone if you haven't learned from life itself or witnessed a situation within your lifetime. I too, like thousands of other lightworkers, was once an apprentice. As I evolved over the years, I had to learn, listen, and grow through my trials and tribulations, just like most of us on this beautiful evolving planet, we call earth. But, as mentioned above, claircognisance also can play a part in helping my clients through their challenging times, by just knowing.

At times, as I am explaining to my clients how to deal with the situation at hand, I'm speaking without knowing what I am going to say until I have actually completed the statement. This I find very incredible, to say the least. I am always amazed and blown away by these types of results. However, if I try to take control of what Spirit is saying through me, I lose what I am supposed to be conveying to my client. I end up sitting in front of them with empty thoughts.

It's times like this when you have to quickly regroup, reverting to being a conduit for Spirit. This means becoming less of me and more of Spirit, remembering that you are the messenger conveying the messages from Spirit energies. On rare occasions, a message can be lost. In these moments, I cherish the lesson learned. However, on the rare occasion when this situation occurs, the message lost will wind its way back into the session a little later throughout the reading. This can be frustrating and amazing at the same time. It's always important to remember to learn from these situations, as it is imperative to stay focused and on track as you continue your journey forward, to be the best medium that you can possibly be.

One significant situation that I have learned is the act of giving and receiving. I once thought, with my old, outdated belief system, that giving and receiving were two different situations. This, I found out the hard way, to be not as I first believed.

This one day in 2010, I had a contract to repaint a general store near my hometown, in the Southern Highlands. I'd been working hard in the heat of summer for a few weeks, prepping and repainting a weatherboard building that looked as though it hadn't been painted for at least twenty years. It was on that hot summer day that I received a phone call from a friend in need of help, with their five-acre manicured garden estate. For personal reasons that I won't go into, my friends asked me if I could help them to get their gardens back into a respectable state of order. I agreed and took a week off work, obliging to help as they had been there for me in past times over the many years that I had known them. I worked tirelessly for a solid week. I had been mowing, whipper-snipping the waist-high grasses and doing whatever else needed attention while giving all that I could. By the week's end, I had depleted my energies, reverting to tapping into my reserve energy storage. I had arrived at the point of exhaustion due to my principal engine running out of steam.

Nearing the final days on the property, I bent over to pick up an armful of grass clippings when my lower back collapsed. I was in excruciating pain from my waist down, leaving me without strength in my legs. I couldn't believe it. I had always been very fit, to the point that

I could keep going and going. However, those days came to an end in one unexpected moment. I was in so much pain that I couldn't stand up under the power of my own strength. I had to use my arms and the strength of my upper body to pull myself up off the ground, onto the side of the trailer, pulling myself up onto the mud-guard, where I sat in total bewilderment and disbelief of what had just occurred. I sat there thinking, *How could this have happened to me?* I felt in a dazed state of mind. I finally got to an area on one of the manicured lawns, with the help of a friend. I laid down upon the earth, under a huge old oak tree, staring up at the summer blue sky while still feeling stunned at what had just taken place, while feeling very concerned.

My Lesson

I then realised that I had given out all of the strength within me, all that I had and more. At the same time, I wasn't thinking of myself at all. This is very typical of a lightworker. I had put myself into a position that threatened my livelihood and all that I had worked so hard for, by gambling with my health.

I had a painting business that I had worked very hard to build up over the previous ten years. How stupid I felt, thinking that I could lose all that I had built and worked so hard for. I did not know the severity of my now condition with my lower back pain, and I wondered how much damage I had caused myself. I had no backup financial plan in place, nothing at all. You know the old saying: "ten feet tall and bulletproof." Always remember that this is just a saying, not a fact.

All this and more had been running through my thoughts while lying there on the manicured lawn as if I were the latest new garden feature from a dollar store. The penny had dropped, during a conversation soon after, about what had just taken place.

I saw in my mind's eye a battery. It was like a AA battery that we use in such tools as a flashlight, with the negative terminal at one end and the positive terminal at the other end. Negative and positive are like yin and yang. When both battery terminals are connected with a wire, a circuit is formed, electricity will then flow through the wire. I realised quite clearly that everything has an opposing situation. Giving has the opposite energy, which is known as receiving.

So now, I look at giving and receiving as a balanced situation, like the image of the AA battery. Just imagine a AA battery with an imaginary electrical circulation of energy pulsating around the outside of itself, continuously—negative to minus and so on. One cannot work without the other.

Try starting your car with the negative cable disconnected from your car battery. Good luck there, I say. If you reconnect the negative cable to the battery, your vehicle will start. One doesn't work without the other. If your car doesn't start, then I would suggest you call roadside assistance.

In the last line that I wrote in the previous paragraph, I shared a touch of my dry sense of humour. However, it actually goes with what I am writing about, within my explanation. For example, you don't have a problem asking for help when your car breaks down, do you? You naturally call for roadside assistance! So why is it so hard to ask for help in other situations? Why does giving seem so easy and effortless a task to do? While receiving seems hard to accept.

If you were to ask for help in any given situation, then you would be *receiving*. The other person would be *giving*. As mentioned in chapter 3, when you genuinely look at it, "giving is a perpetual situation that needs a recipient to complete the circle of energy." As the AA battery needs a positive side, it will only work as it should with a recipient end, which is the negative side, therefore completing the circle of energy and thus working as it was initially intended.

Next time a lending hand is graciously offered by another, who wants to gift something to you or provide you with assistance totally unconditionally, make it easy on yourself and wipe that nervous sweat from your brow, replying with a statement of gratitude, such as, "Thank you," stating, "Yes, your help would be appreciated." You will witness the worthiness within yourself light up, creating a feeling of happiness and gratitude for both the recipient and the receiver.

You are inadvertently helping the other person by accepting their offer of service when that person reaches out to offer you help.

The act of giving is something that the generous person could be struggling with. As mentioned, there is always an opposing energy. However, from experience, I believe that the act of receiving, rather than giving, is the one thing mankind struggles with on average. The action of giving seems to be a smoother transaction to undertake, resonating with ease. As you begin to receive, you begin to build and exercise your muscle of self-worth.

I have met many people who can give until the cows come home, which is great if you live on a dairy farm. But when it is time for a person to receive, they struggle with this situation that is placed upon them. This can be due to how we are brought up—for example, by our parents, or by teachings taught to us through society. Another reason is that your self-worth may be at rock bottom as you refuse to believe that you are worthy of receiving at all. Simply put, you may want to save the world, wanting nothing for yourself, which, to a degree, is okay. However, keep in mind the harmonious balance of the AA battery energies.

Lightworkers must also recognise the opposing energies of being a lightworker, understanding that the opposite energy is to be a dark-worker. I'm not saying to be evil or anything of that nature, just that we should recognise balance by merely taking time out to fill up our own energy tank. Remember, nothing runs on empty.

Try driving your vehicle one thousand kilometres on one tank of fuel. You are not going to arrive at your chosen holiday destination. You will break down, running out of fuel before you reach your desired beachside resort. You have to stop and refuel. Then you can continue on your journey.

We can't go around giving all that we have. If we focus all our energies on giving, then we will collapse in a heap, as I pointed out in a previous paragraph. If we let ourselves only give and give and give, then soon our batteries will be running on empty. At that time, we will be of no use to anyone and indeed not of any good to humanity at all.

Balancing your energies is totally necessary. Be selfish every now and then; be kind to yourself every now and then. You know that you are allowed to be. You have earned the privilege! When you have had your fill and replenished your energies, then you can jump right back into the humanitarian ring for another bout of servitude to mankind.

But when you hear those warning signals, listen to those warnings as a signal to then be kind to yourself once again and replenish your energies. Take the necessary time to recharge yourself, sitting in the same circle of the perpetual giving that I mentioned previously. (Perpetual giving also requires a receiver to complete the circle of energy.)

Traits of a Lightworker

Lightworkers are souls working towards bringing healing, love, and compassion to the world, who have incarnated here on earth to be of divine service to mankind and all living things. This is not a new trend here on earth—far from it.

Lightworkers have been here on earth since the dawn of time. I have noticed over the past few years that there are more and more lightworkers emerging, venturing out into the public eye, spreading their healing light to those less fortunate. It is also fantastic that now there are celebrities who have bravely become open with their abilities, reaching out to thousands of more people in need of healing and direction, using tools such as TV, newspapers, magazines, and now also, in a vast way, social media—all reaching out, enlightening the public on the world stage. This, in turn, has encouraged many other lightworkers throughout the world to walk bravely amongst humanity, as they begin to own their abilities, shedding light on to humanity with their own uniqueness and choice of modalities. The skills that I have personally witnessed stem from clairvoyants, mediums, healers, shamans, and angel workers, just to name a few. However, there are far more than this. A local optometrist travels to impoverished countries to help people with eye conditions. I believe that there is a group that goes together to achieve this. Or perhaps you have heard of doctors travelling to Third World countries to heal the sick. A taxi driver can also be seen as a lightworker, as he transports the elderly every other week to take them to the supermarket so they can purchase their groceries; while engaging in general conversation as the taxi driver offers assistance with the heavy load of groceries.

However, these are the modalities with which we are all very familiar. The not-so-familiar lightworkers, which we don't seem to recognise, can include beauticians, care-givers, charity workers, volunteers, nurses, doctors, or those who commit selfless acts of kindness by paying for the next person's coffee at a cafe. There are many more examples of this, right down to someone who gives away their money to a homeless person on the streets, in turn, helping them with a little kindness and understanding, making their street life a little more comfortable. These are the few examples that I have personally witnessed throughout the years.

Just last week, I had a coffee at the local Rocca Café here in my home town, with my client and friend, Di. I saw a man sitting by himself at one of the outside tables, across from where Di and myself were chatting over a coffee. He seemed very content and somehow familiar to me, even though I had never met him before. The man, as I found out later, was a Qantas captain, not that you would actually guess his profession by looking at him. He said hello to Di from the front of the cafe. The traffic noise combined with my rock 'n roll–related hearing difficulties made it difficult to hear what the man was saying to Di.

The friend of Di's went inside and paid his bill. On the way out, he gestured his goodbyes to Di and me. Di and I continued our conversation until the time came for her to attend her business meeting. I then went inside to pay for our coffees. But as I went to pay, I was told at the counter that the bill for our beverages had already been paid for.

I stood there bewildered and quickly worked out what had taken place. Di's friend, the Qantas captain, had generously paid our cafe bill. I thought, *How cool is that!* I was amazed, as I always am when witnessing kindness from another person. The man didn't know me at all. (However, I could understand him paying for Di.)

The man's kindness felt great. It was an excellent feeling to receive a kind gesture such as this. It just goes to show that it's not that difficult to be kind to someone, whether you know them or not. It shows that it also isn't that difficult to spread kindness amongst humanity. It certainly is a good feeling when kindness happens to you.

Was the man that paid for our coffee, in my eyes, a lightworker? The answer is yes. I very much believe this to be so. In fact, in my eyes, he is definitely a lightworker. Will I ever see this man again to say thank you and perhaps return the kind gesture shown to me? The answer is probably not. However, I can pay it forward in my own ways! This kind gesture also explains how to think differently, with a lesson attached to "paying-forward", that to be selflessly giving to another person, would be an excellent feeling for the recipient to experience, in turn, making their day, just that little bit brighter. This will also open their eyes to paying-forward, offering a gesture of kindness to an unsuspecting member of society. To me, it is all one step closer to world peace.

It only took one droplet of water to create the ocean, same as it only takes one person to start a war. Just imagine pouring that negative warlike energy into a more productive, positive type of venture. It shows that anything and everything is possible. The same as one cup of coffee handed to a complete stranger could be the beginning of obtaining world peace, spreading kindness amongst our fellow man.

Empaths

How do you know if you are an empath?

An empath is very sensitive to the emotions of people and living things around them, no matter how small. Empathic people can profoundly feel other people's moods and emotions, sometimes mistaking the energies for their own. As very sensitive people, empaths will absorb the negativity of others by taking on the negative energy as there own. This is very unintentional. Walking into a room after an argument has taken place, an empath can pick up on any lingering negative energy residue.

Have you ever been in a fantastic mood, maybe walking downtown on a bright, harmonious sunny day, just minding your own business while taking in the sights and smells on your travels; then, out of nowhere, you begin to feel down, a feeling as if you were depressed, with negative thoughts replacing the happy thoughts of that vibrant, sunny day stroll that you had witnessed moments before?

The explanation may be that you are an empathic person and very sensitive to your surroundings. What has just taken place to make you feel this way? The answer is quite likely that you have just absorbed someone else's negative energy and made it your own, without actually realising it.

Being an empath is like being a human sponge, soaking up the negative energies of the world around you. At the same time, you may not truly understand why this is happening to you, which makes life a little unbearable at times, not only for you but for the people around you who care deeply for you, witnessing your struggles. In your mind sits a ball of confusion, while you keep asking yourself, time after time: What is wrong with me? This is a great question!

One of my favourite John Holland quotes is "Instead of asking yourself, 'What is wrong with me?' ask yourself, 'Who is wrong with me?'"

Once you have the understanding that you are an empath (also known as "a sensitive"), you will see that your empathic side has been controlling you, when in fact you should be managing your empathic side. As you begin to realise what is wrong with you, you begin to see what is right with you—that being an empath is a positive side of you instead of being burdensome to you.

Leading up to your inner awakening, you will begin to see the answers you've been asking yourself for many years. You may have, at times, felt like an outsider, or your peers may have considered you different. You may have questioned yourself often throughout the years, "What is my life's purpose?" The more you take time out to discover the workings of *you*, the more that you will discover what your life's purpose truly is.

My question to you is "What is your passion?" What do you love to do where the hours burn away at the blink of an eye? When you have the answer to that burning question, this will most likely lead you to your life's purpose—or at the very least, lead you to the threshold for you to begin your journey towards a definite life's purpose.

Empaths tend to be drawn to creative expressions, such as composing music, writing, poetry, painting, acting, and the performing arts. Within the vibrations of the arts contains expressions of healing, which can inadvertently become a tool of healing for the recipient while reaping the rewards from the enjoyment of the arts.

The vibration of music, along with the written word, can, for example, help you through downtimes. I have witnessed this on stage many times over the years while singing and performing as a member of a band. Sometimes, I would see a lost soul out in the audience as I was performing on stage, and I would deliberately deliver a line out of a song directly to that lost soul, pushing my energies out into the audience, transporting a message of peace and harmony. The power of a microphone can reach and heal many.

Have you ever had a down day and then cranked your music-listening device all the way up to eleven? Did you then notice, almost instantaneously, that now you were suddenly starting to feel happier within?

I see, that the vibrating sound of music when played in a room breaks down the negative energies consuming that particular space, that is within you and the said room. The vibration of sound, therefore, breaks up into thousands of tiny particles, dispersing the negative energy out into the atmosphere. It's another form of cleansing the soul, which is also a form of sound healing.

Music lifts the soul, pouring light into the darker moments within our lives, creating the magical power of healing. The lyrics of songs and the words of poetry can resonate powerfully, providing the magic healing words that pour new light and wisdom into the listener's ears or the reader's eyes.

Take, for instance, this book that I am writing. I felt a calling to write this book, to help you and others out in the world who may be struggling to understand what they are going through, psychically or otherwise. It is my hope to make your journey that little bit easier for you to see and understand. I had begun to write a journal on my psychic experiences. I never really had a complete plan of writing a book at this early stage in my career. It came about through a series of divine events that prompted me to begin writing now. Therefore, the best thing that you can do in this situation is to listen, have faith, and trust in oneself and the divine energies to take pen in hand and start writing.

I'm writing this book straight from the heart, so I know that it will benefit all who read it in some way. *Student of the Universe*, metaphorically speaking, can be likened to a drop of water. The ocean was created one drop at a time. Each and every one of us is a "student of the universe."

When we are born to this world, we aren't delivered with our very own troubleshooting manual, clutched in our tiny little hands. Nor was any personnel manual bestowed upon us in the maternity ward as a bonus for making it to Earth. We write our owner's manuals as we traverse through life, matching our own uniquenesses, as we live uniquely, through each and every day. Birth is the beginning of our "apprenticeship," as we learn and evolve into the best person that we can possibly be until our spiritual awakening date arrives.

Spiritual Awakening

There are many informational versions and individual meanings to the title of "spiritual awakening." The title could also be referred to as "inner awakening." I will do my best to explain my personal take on this subject.

There is really no one answer to what spiritual awakening actually means, because we are all individuals, transcending through our own personal growth and spiritual transformations.

Just as the Pacific Ocean extends from the Arctic Ocean in the north, up and down the West Coast of America, to the southern ocean in the south, the Atlantic Ocean is bound on the east by North and South America, which connects to the Arctic Ocean. These two oceans are in different parts of the world, separated by giant landmasses. The common ground, though, is that they possess the same makeup of water, marine life, flora and fauna beneath the surface.

So, yes, there are common symptoms that you will experience as you go through your spiritual awakening. We may encounter all or some of these symptoms. However, the end result is the beginning of your spiritual modality of choice—being of service to mankind, spreading love and light throughout the world as we step closer to world peace through our positive actions of love and light.

There are many triggers to set you off on your spiritual path, such as losing a loved one. Losing one who is dear to you can encourage you to delve deep to find the answers to the questions that linger in your mind, such as "What is life really about?" It may seem unfair at times to see someone you care about—whether its a friend, family member or life partner—depart from this earth. But the knowledge and understanding that we are spiritual energy, experiencing a human life, help you to understand that your loved ones have transitioned to another world, that they are still very much around you, albeit in a nonphysical form.

The simple fact is I believe that we are here on earth as souls experiencing a human life, to be the best person that we can possibly be by evolving, learning, and unconditionally spreading love and light among mankind. In turn, this brings us one step closer to world peace. I believe this is all a part of a soul's journey. Once you have experienced your spiritual awakening, you must own your gifts, abilities, and uniqueness, using the gift of modalities that suit you, understanding that your spiritual awakening is the beginning of a new chapter in your life.

Understand, though, that you are unique, with your own signs, symbols, and ways of intuitive learning. It's a good idea to start a journal, creating your personal meanings for your signs and symbols. Some signs and symbols will be familiar, such as a white feather floating seemingly straight in a gust of wind, as if held by someone or somebody invisible to the naked eye. This symbol could mean that you are protected, that your guardian angels are with you at your time of need.

Ten signs that a lightworker may experience during spiritual awakening.

1. **Empathy.** You possess a desire to make the world a better place by creating a positive impact on the world, which includes mankind, animals, and the planet.
2. **Sensitivity.** Your emotions become much more sensitive. Your senses, sight, taste, smell, feeling, hearing all become much more heightened, along with your intuition increasing in sensitivity, whereas you become more guided, embracing your intuition.
3. **Creativity.** You become more creative and inspired by music, the performing arts, painting, and writing, along with other creative inspirations. Creativity is encouraged and performs straight from the heart (your emotions).

4. **Intuition.** You begin to just *know* certain events while fully trusting in what you are sensing. You feel, hear, and see from a higher perspective. Gradually, your intuition becomes stronger as you learn and understand how to grow with your intuition. Trusting in your intuition is the hardest lesson; however, from trial and error, you will fine-tune your heightened ability.

5. **Synchronicities.** Synchronicities begin to take place, such as seeing repeating numbers. The most common numbers at the beginning of your awakening stage are the numbers 11:11, 3:33, 2:22, and 4:44. These numbers are known as *angel numbers*. Many interpretations of the angel numbers can be found online. Likewise, as mentioned in a previous chapter, there are many books on this subject. One of my favourite books is *"Angel Numbers 101"* by Doreen Virtue.

6. **Sleep patterns.** It seems that no matter how much sleep you get, you remain tired and fatigued. Don't worry. It won't last forever. (Also, check with your doctor if this is a problem.) You may also notice that you tend to wake up at certain times throughout the night. These times of awakening are usually around 2:22, 3:33, and 4:44 in the morning.

7. **Lack of concern.** You have a lack of worries, conflicts, and judgment or fear-based concerns, transitioning your energies to more love-based energy. This is a state of being, changing the way that you usually see situations. To "just be" sounds like an easy thing to accomplish and understand. On the contrary: something so simple is not so easy, and yet it is. This seems to be a paradox, but this is all apart of the process of being unconditional. Once you reach this enlightenment stage, you will understand why I say it's very simple to "just be."

8. **Unconditional love.** You help and serve all life, totally unconditionally and without judgement, regardless of a being's race, size, or species. We begin to see how we are all equal.

9. **Universal connectivity.** You connect with the universe and all living things, using your abilities for the betterment of mankind and all living things.

10. **Contentment.** You feel content, happy, balanced, and structured, having a strong connection with animals and plants, our planet, and, of course, mankind.

The list of ten awakening symptoms are very similar, and all blend into each other to become one. These are just a few symptoms that I experienced over the years. There are many more symptoms that you will undergo, as you will come to realise as you grow with your spiritual awakening.

I suggest that you go with the flow, don't be in a hurry, while at the same time enjoying your journey. If you have any questions about your path at all, remember, that we are always the student, so the teacher will appear when the student is in need. Question all that puzzles you by attending, courses, workshops and the study of books. I found that blogs and vlogs found on online platforms can sometimes hold the answers to your queries.

I suggest that you also attend an array of mediumship platforms by well known or highly recommended mediums, so that you may understand, the workings of mediumship. John Holland, John Edward, and Gordon Smith are some of my many favourite mediums. They have been working in their fields for decades, while leading the way, to bring psychic work and mediumship to the public, in a more accepted way.

I never stop learning. Never stop evolving. Never stop on the journey of spreading love, light, and healing to mankind. But most of all, be humble and stay protected and grounded while trusting in yourself and the road that you're on. All at the steady pace of one step at a time.

CHAPTER 5

PASSION AND PURPOSE

Begin now, live your life to the nth degree with passion. Find what it is that really excites you, and there, you will find your life's purpose.

—Doc O'Toole

We are all born into this world with a soul purpose. Our purpose in life is unique for each individual. As part of your life's purpose, you must find exactly what that purpose may be. It may take years to reach this stage of your life while you are here on earth, as so many before us have found. I believe that an individuals life purpose begins at birth. The discovery of why you are here and what you are here to achieve, at any level, will arrive at the precise time that it should. This is known as divine timing, in which your life's purpose may come to you early in your life or much later. Whichever applies to you, patience must be exercised as you live out a healthy everyday existence, enjoying the experiences and pleasantries that this world has to offer.

I have met lots of people and have performed many psychic readings for clients who are searching for the reason they have incarnated here on earth. At the same time, they are looking for their specific answers to explain why they are here in this beautiful world. If you think about it, the querent has arrived at these questions: "Why am I here?" and "What is my life's purpose?" These questions appear at precisely the right time of an individual's awakening stage of their life. This is mainly because of their own personal, individual journey, which began from the time of their birth to the time of their self-questioning of, "what is my life purpose", therefore, becoming more seriously focused and involved in their own personal life purpose here on earth. I believe that they are now beginning to listen to their internal voice, their intuition, which some call the "gut feeling."

Usually, we become inquisitive when life throws us a curveball or some kind of tragedy occurs, such as the loss of a loved one. This will set the questions in motion, seemingly waking you from a deep sleep with a feeling of vividly, stepping out into the world for the first time. It takes one spark within your comfortable lifestyle to push you outside your comfort zone. It's a voice, a yearning feeling inside of you, that forces you to search outside yourself, which is out of your comfort zone, as you find yourself saying, "There must be more to life than this?"

We have to travel along our personal highway to experience a particular sequence of events, to grow and to learn so that we may evolve into our life's purpose. We are precisely where we are supposed to be at any given time. Yes, we may indeed experience a wrong turn while making bad choices every now and then. Trial and error are how humans evolve and learn. This is the free will part of us. I believe that this is all about learning and growing, becoming the student and then becoming the teacher while retaining the attitude of the student.

Every day, more and more people in the world are reaching their awakening stage. It's not until you start researching metaphysics, via books, websites, and most of all these days, social media platforms, that you will truly understand your awakening. The number of people out there in this world spreading love and light through their own modalities is astonishing. I would like to personally take the time, at this very moment, to thank you all for your work and dedication. Thank you for stepping outside of comfort zone, for becoming a part of the thousands of other lightworkers, adding that drop of water to the ocean of life. Remember, it's not a competition. We are all working together.

Staying humble while unconditionally spreading light and love, adding healing to the world, is what life is truly about.

From a young age, I have always felt different from anyone else. I have always thought that I was the black sheep, but I never quite knew why. However, at the same time, I had always felt that I had a specific life's purpose of fulfilling. I also never questioned what that purpose might be, as I quietly and knowingly trusted that someday, I would find what my life's purpose was while living out my life. I never quite knew what my difference was all about or what my purpose was in the larger scheme of things, but I have always been keenly aware of my surroundings. Somehow, I always seemed to know what was happening, even if a situation was hidden or kept from me. I could always read the room, so to speak. I could walk into a room and sum it up very quickly, getting a sense of whom to trust and whom not to trust. If I felt I didn't belong in that room or restaurant, I would leave, believing my internal intuitive alarm.

Just before I turned eighteen, I applied to enter the Royal Australian Navy. I had been very excited about this new destination in my life. I had applied for marine technical hull and also an underwater photographer as my chosen profession. I'd always loved the ocean and still do. To me, the ocean holds a certain kind of magical healing and a cleansing vibration. After visiting the coastal waters, either scuba diving, swimming or strolling along the sandy shoreline, I feel so revitalised and cleansed. While scuba diving, I love to lie at the bottom of the ocean, at around twenty meters or so, on a bright sunny day, where the visibility is just over twenty-five meters. I would take the regulator out of my mouth while lying at the bottom of the ocean, then blow air from my mouth, creating huge water rings. Lying there at the bottom of the ocean, I would watch the water rings increase in size as they made their way to the glistening surface of the sea.

About one week before I was to leave my home town to have my medical examination by the RAN, I was involved in a severe motorcycle accident. One late winter afternoon, around 5:00 p.m., I was riding my Honda motorcycle along the main road in my home town. I remember riding along when I noticed a car stationary giving way to me, waiting to turn right over a railway bridge. In my mind, and visually, the driver of the vehicle was giving way to me, as he should have. However, when I was about a car's length from the driver, with the driver thinking that he had enough time, he decided he would turn right over the railway bridge, voiding his giving way to me far too late. The driver of the vehicle had left me no time at all for any evasive action. The collision happened in slow motion, with nowhere to escape the impending accident, which was over in a matter of seconds.

The next thing I knew, the driver of the car had T-boned me, driving his vehicle into the side of my bike, crushing my right leg in the process. I lay there on the asphalt, looking up to see if my motorcycle was okay. You know—as you do! My bike was fine, without much damage at all. I started to check to see if I had any injuries. Hmm—a resounding yes in my mind was the result of that question, along with some other words to comfort me. I won't go into too much detail, but my leg, where the driver T-boned me, had suffered a severe compound fracture. It wasn't a pretty sight. The ambulance arrived, and so did my new future, all in the same afternoon, as I celebrated at the local hospital, toasting to my new future with morphine that evening, with the hopes of killing the most intense, excruciating pain I'd ever experienced.

As I lay in the hospital for a couple of months, a very skilled specialist, Dr Harbison, managed to reconstruct and save my leg, which included three skin graft operations. I had to learn to walk with the aid of a walking frame and physiotherapy. I soon realised that my future in the Royal Australian Navy was not to be. The universe had retired me from the RAN way before I set sail on my chosen destination.

By the time I had arrived home from the hospital, though I still had a long way to go, I was well on the road to healing. Although my life was forever changed by this event, I had survived the traumatic ordeal, which today I'm very grateful for.

With the confirmation that I wouldn't be joining the Royal Australian Navy due to my physical injury, my lifelong dream became another dream.

Taking it all in my stride, believing that the accident had all happened for a reason, I sat in my favourite chair, with my fully plastered leg elevated. I began to think of other options for what I could do with my life. I had always been very ambitious, so it never occurred to me to just sit around or work in a factory for the rest of my life. Not that there is anything wrong with working in a factory; it just wasn't what I aspired to be. However, I did receive an offer to join the RAN as general entry, but by this stage, my heart was no longer in it, so I declined the offer.

That same day that the RAN offered me the option of general entry while sitting in my favourite chair, I decided that I would become a professional musician. I played the guitar at the time—sang and wrote a little too. I had been very passionate about rock 'n roll and would daydream about performing on stage in front of thousands of fans.

To this day, being on stage, performing a favourite song to a packed audience gives me excited butterflies in my stomach. So, off I ventured to the starting position of a new career, travelling on a very long and winding road, becoming a member of the society of rock 'n roll. I started learning more about the musical craft, bettering myself so that I could become the best musician that I aspired to be.

I started taking guitar lessons and travelling two hours for singing lessons to Strobek Music, in Brookvale, a suburb on the north side of Sydney. I also created my first rock band with my good friend, Mac. He was also very talented and a great rhythm player. With Mac's brother on drums, I had my first band. During one of our first rehearsals, with the "No-Name Band," while playing the guitar, I stopped and headed towards the microphone that we had set up. I was strongly drawn to becoming a vocalist. It had felt so right. So from that day on, I began the life of a singer-songwriter.

About two years after my first band, in 1985, I received an offer to join my first professional band, with seasoned musicians. The new group, Murphy's Law, was a great learning curve for me. The boys were totally seasoned professionals, which I found excellent, as I became the weak link in the band, which to me was a great position to be in. Being the weak link in the band or any situation gave me room to grow to the level of my bandmates.

A mutual friend of Murphy's Law had heard me singing with my "No-Name Band," which I had created with Mac and his brother. This mutual friend then introduced me to the band Murphy's Law, who had been looking for a frontman. As a member of Murphy's Law, I also was delighted to get the opportunity to record my first professional recordings.

Moving on from Murphy's Law, I joined a few other bands and jammed with friends, each time learning and growing. I had also become a roadie for major bands touring through my home town. I enjoyed this process, as I was learning the workings of production and sound. I wanted to know everything so that I could become self-sufficient.

A vocalist from an Australian rock band, Richard (not his real name), who lived not too far from me, had been kind enough to share his musical knowledge with me. I rode up to the home where Richard lived at the time, as I had been on a mission to pick the brains of someone who had been there, done that, and bought the T-shirt.

Richard was very hospitable and accommodating. He offered me some simple and powerful advice, which for an eighteen-year-old was very valuable information. I then carried with me this newfound knowledge, throughout the many years to come, in my chosen career as a singer-songwriter. Kindly, Richard also invited me to come along to rehearsals and such, but I never did. I cherished the information that he gave me as I set about carving out my own, rock 'n roll career. So, with this newfound information from the generosity of Richard, I ventured off, travelling my new journey along the rock 'n roll highway.

In the late eighties, I packed up my belongings and moved to Sydney. I had joined the rock 'n roll limelights of Sydney, becoming the vocalist/frontman for a well-known hard rock band, Fire and Ice. I had felt so at home with this band, I just loved being a part of a group of like-minded musicians. We had management and were supporting major acts, such as "De' Mont" and "The Bombers," as well as other well-known bands of that time. I couldn't believe that I had made it this far within the music industry. I had jumped into the deep end, and I was swimming hard and fast, with total focus and dedication, living and breathing rock 'n roll.

It seemed that my destination had been laid out for me. Although there were some hard times, I enjoyed every minute of being a musician. For many years, I had felt like an outsider, always looking in, never truly belonging anywhere, but with the music industry, I had found a home of like-minded people. I had been a member of many bands over the years of both cover bands and original bands, always looking to create the ultimate show. I had created and joined a few original bands over the years. With each band, I would put 150 percent into each project, each rehearsal, and each and every live show, giving it all I had at each event that I performed at.

Down on my luck in the early nineties, I didn't have enough money for a meal each day, which caused me to become unwell with malnutrition. The soup kitchen was suggested to me a few times, but I had declined that suggestion, thinking that this type of service had been set up for the people that were down and out, who were having a hard time at that stage of their lives.

Just thinking about that last sentence as I'm typing here, I'm having a laugh to myself, thinking, *Yes that service was also for me. I was down and out, too!* Sometimes that's not how I think or feel. I knew that there were many other people out there in this world much worse off than I was. Knowing and thinking this way keeps you active and pointed in the right direction.

I decided to create a concept show. This was against my better judgment, as I really wanted to be apart of an original band. I needed to feed myself and keep a roof over my head, so I formed the band, "Circus Animals," performing the classic songs by a well-known Australian band. Even though I can sing most songs directed at me, I was more of an original artist, wanting to achieve my ultimate band to fulfil myself artistically, ultimately achieving success as an original artist.

Towards the end of the 1990s, Richard's band was reforming after many years. A friend, Shay (not her real name), who was one of the backing vocalists for the upcoming tour, contacted me on my mobile phone as I was on my way from Strathfield to an out-of-town gig. She asked me if I would like to do the upcoming tour. I was floored. I responded, *"Yes,* when do we leave?" Shay had a laugh, expressing that she knew this would be my answer. I thought she must be psychic. Shay went on to explain that I would have to do an audition at 10:00 a.m. the next morning, at Stage Door Productions. There would be no time to revise the songs. I had to perform a cold audition.

The next day, at Stage Door Productions, I arrived with little to no sleep under my belt due to the excitement. I was also still on a high after the gig the night before, and I had slept on a mate's uncomfortable lounge. At this stage, it did not matter. Whatever was thrown at me, I was ready to rock.

Shay met me as I arrived at Stage Door and led me upstairs to where she had a vocal PA set up, with two boom mics and a tape of the songs ready, that I was to perform vocal harmonies too. During the audition, I wondered how I might be doing. I glanced over at Shay, who was on the second microphone. To my surprise, she was looking back at me with a big glowing smile on her face. I thought, *Great! I must be doing okay— Very cool, I thought!* After the audition, Shay took me into her office to explain the circumstances. She said that the lead singer Richard, had been looking for his usual backing vocalist for the upcoming tour and that I would be on standby for the backing vocalist position if they needed me. I thought, *Damn! There's a catch?*

About a week after my audition, on a Sunday afternoon, Shay contacted me to say that Richards had found the backing vocalist he had been searching for. I was obviously a little disappointed, but at the same time, I was delighted that I had even been considered for the job. It was also a personal gauge of where I stood as a vocalist amongst my peers. After all the years of hard work, building my vocals to a professional state of musicianship, I had earned respect from a vocalist whom I looked up to. Thank you, Shay, for your consideration. It meant the world to me.

However, the most incredible thing about this audition was that it was Richard, all those years ago, who had taken the time and the effort to speak with me, offering "rock 'n roll guidance" to a young, inexperienced singer who was starting out on his personal journey. He showed consideration to a young eighteen-year-old, with a mindset determined to be successful, while kindly giving me a direction to head in. He had led me to water, pointing me north; the rest was up to me. I thought, *wow, I have come full circle.*

There have been many life lessons throughout my music career, along with mentors offering words of wisdom, some known and some not so well known. It does not matter where the teachings and mentoring hail from. To me, we all learn and grow together, evolving for the betterment of mankind. With Richard and other musicians that I have gained knowledge from, to me, it is the same as learning from a master mechanic wanting to build that ultimate machine, learning and evolving from the lessons of others who have had the experience in a chosen situation or field of expertise. I, in turn, have since passed my experience on to others, paying it forward, whether teaching guitar or teaching vocals or applying my newfound knowledge to anyone struggling to move forward within their own personal life or career. This includes standing on stage and speaking on the topic of metaphysics. I have seen that a particular lesson I may have received from a specific field of expertise can be adapted for many other areas of proficiency as well, even applied to problematic day-to-day situations.

Life became harder, living in Sydney. I had become homeless. I sometimes had the pleasure of sleeping on a mate's lounge for the night, although I mostly lived in my car, boon-docking by a river's edge, sleeping at industrial complexes, or sleeping at twenty-four-hour fuel stations. I could feel myself heading towards a breakdown, which eventually did come.

The universe had been nudging me to move back to my hometown, but I kept unintentionally resisting the move. Eventually, the universe came down heavy on me, forcing me altogether to move away from the city. I had always loved the city life, but it was time to move on. Thank God! Because, by this stage, I was burnt out. At the same time, I was making way for my impending breakdown.

I headed back to my home town to visit an old friend, James. James was and still is, to this day, a great friend. He could see that I needed help and opened up his home to me. The funny thing is I was so not of this planet at the time, so I didn't see what James was up to at first. I would have refused his generosity if I had been in a better frame of mind.

James, at the time, had a painter and decorator business, which was also my trade. I started working for James, who also was responsible for me getting back into my profession, getting me back on track and therefore giving me a solid foundation to recuperate, thus beginning a new chapter in my life. "Just looking after a friend," as he would say.

A few months later, James rang another painter who he had completed his apprenticeship through years earlier and landed me a job as a subcontract painter. I spent the next two years working as a subcontractor, getting my skills back up until I eventually started my own business. I am so very grateful to James, Cliff, and others who supported me through those trying times, giving me a leg up and a chance to get back up on my feet, to live life again.

While I was working as a subcontractor, my grandfather had passed away from cancer. Pop always wanted me to repaint his home, but this never happened. This was for the simple reason that I wanted to paint his house free of charge, but Pop wished to pay me for my work. So, there was a loving standoff between us, which is something that I cherish.

After my grandfather had passed, with his home now sold, I received a phone call on a Thursday, around noon, while still subcontracting for Cliff. It happened to be the PA for my accountant. She asked me if I could schedule a time to do a quote for a home that my accountant had purchased. Somehow, I just knew it was Pop's old home that had been purchased. I said to the PA, "Is the address number five Fitzroy Street?" The PA was stunned. She asked me with curiosity about how I knew this information. I replied, "That's my grandfather's home." I never really explained how I knew, but the truth is that I heard the information in my mind. I knew, without a doubt, that what I was hearing was correct.

This wasn't the first time I had heard information, either in my mind or through a disembodied voice. However, this time it was close to home. Pop definitely had the last say with our quandary, while also proving to me that his spirit still lived, that only his body had died. This memory and experience I hold dear to my heart. Every now and then, when that experience appears in my thoughts, I have a quiet laugh to myself, saying, "Hi, Pop. How are you? Yeah, I know, you had the last word."

Pop didn't mind a drink or two. A few months before he passed, I went to visit him in the hospital. On the way, I stopped off and bought him a small bottle of beer. His eyes lit up like overcoat buttons when I presented him with the golden beverage. I cracked the top and passed him his beer. He downed it as if he had just walked through the desert and was dying of thirst, as he drank every last bit of the amber liquid.

Pop once told me of a story of his friend, who was dying from lung cancer. His friend had been a heavy smoker throughout his life. One day, towards the end of his friend's life, Pop went to visit his friend in the hospital. Knowing that his friend didn't have long to live, he bought his mate a packet of cigarettes. This story told to me by my grandfather is what prompted me to purchase him that ice-cold beer for him that day. I'm so glad that I did. It has left a lasting and memorable impression in my thoughts, always leaving a smile on my face.

I know that Pop and other loved ones are still around me. In fact, Pop is with me at this very moment. As I sat down to write more of this chapter, I had intended to write about something totally opposite, but as I began to write, the story of Pop arrived in my thoughts. So, I typed away.

His presence is a validation of love and the hearing of his words, which I hear as I type: "I'm proud of you, son," he says. When I think of Pop, I smile. My heart fills with love for him. In my eyes, he was such a great man.

It's validations like this that we all should be aware of. It sounds too simple and too good to be true. But the truth is that it *is* true. The fact is our bodies are a vehicle to carry our souls through this life while here on earth. We cannot die. Only the vehicle that transports us around here on earth dies. Our soul is energy, and energy cannot be destroyed.

It wasn't long after getting a fresh start with my health and beginning my painting business that my next band was born. "The Rock Show Australia", as the band was called, came together quite quickly. An old friend, Kevin Lucas, gave me a call one night while I was laying down some tracks in my home studio. Kev's always been a good friend to me and everyone, but we had a special connection. I guess that we both came from the same background of music and loved bands such as Whitesnake, Van Halen, and Led Zeppelin, who all come from the same school of rock.

We loved all the classic rock arena bands. While Kev is a great guitarist, he could also play all the classic tunes very well. My voice and vocal range perfectly matched Kev's playing abilities. During our general phone conversation, Kev mentioned that he wasn't performing with a band. Naturally, I responded, "Neither am I." The next minute, we were saying, "Okay, let's do something together." That night, Kev and I became the founding members of The Rock Show Australia.

Kev and I decided to put a concept band together. We created a concept performing all the classic rock songs from the 70s through to the early 90s. Within a month, we were all rehearsed, with posters, website, gigs lined up, and a cracking band with a powerful rhythm section. We hit the road a little over a month after that late-night phone call from Kev.

Instantly we had a following. It was absolutely amazing. The support and loyalty we received from our fans were incredible. If you are reading this and were one of those loyal fans, I thank you from the bottom of my heart. Without people like you, there would be no bands. The Rock Show Australia attracted people with special needs and other disabilities. We would take good care of these people and took time out to make a fuss over them. This was something that I personally enjoyed. Music is healing, in many ways, on all levels.

The Rock Show Australia performed every weekend. Sometimes I finished work early on a Thursday, travelled to Sydney to do a gig, then down to Wagga, performing a concert at Goulburn on the way back, then to Parramatta on a Sunday night, clocking up many kilometres over a long weekend tour, to get ready for work on Monday. With every show, I put in 150 percent, no matter how tired I was at the time.

I remember showing up to a client's home on a Monday morning, ready to put in a hard day's work. Maggie came to the door, surprised that I had even shown up after the previous long weekend tour. She took one look at me and said, "What are you doing here? Go home and sleep." I was so glad that particular time that Maggie ordered me home to rest. I was dead on my feet but ready to work just the same. She was very understanding and to this day remains very supportive of me.

I really enjoyed being a member of The Rock Show Australia, and I met a lot of great people along the way. After about three years with the band, I started to get the yearning to create my original band. My intuition had been directing me to move on. I was torn between two worlds, two roads, and I decided to leave the band that Kev and I had created. I spoke to Kev, explaining my quandary, that I had to do the original band thing. That my heart and soul had been pulling me into a new creative direction. Thankfully, Kev understood.

We had a few more obligations over the next few months, with venues booked, but after they were fulfilled, The Rock Show Australia was put to bed. Kev didn't want another vocalist to join. We had a brotherly connection with complementary musical chemistry on stage. We would bounce off each other and complemented each other as a guitarist and vocalist should. Sometimes that chemistry is hard to match up in bands, but when it does match up, it's bloody fantastic, and that's when the magic happens.

I waisted no time creating my project, The Red Dragon band, in late 2005. I knew exactly what direction I wanted to go in and the sound I wanted to achieve. I created demos and paid for them to be professionally constructed. I created a demo CD and set about looking for band members. With the demo CD, I could shop my idea around to find like-minded musicians, hoping they could add to the band and add there own personal touches to my CD of demo songs, bringing their own unique styles to the table. I had planted the seed, and now I needed it to blossom and grow.

Many times, I had been let down along the way while in search of band members. I would find a suitable guitarist or drummer, who would seem very keen, and then they would fade away. Time after time, this would happen. Eventually, several years on, I gave up. I had become very disillusioned with the music industry. I had given all that I had over many years to create a creative and successful career. I guess the writing was on the wall!

Finally, I came to a decision to retire from performing with bands. These days, however, I jam in my home studio or have a jam night around at mates' home. However, it seemed to me that my life was changing. A lot of things and situations would leave my life over the next while. My relationship with my fiancée ended, and a good friend passed from cancer all in a very short space of time, which rocked me to the core. I struggled to understand what was happening to me as I spiralled into depression mode while witnessing my life beeing about-faced and turned upside down.

I couldn't understand what was going on. I had always known where I was headed, where I was going, and how I would achieve this. The day-in and day-out routine had become a struggle for me. Going through depression is a long and hard road, as many of you may understand. It took all my strength to get up every morning and go to work, to function through my regular daily routine.

Hiding my depression became more manageable as the years went on, and I eventually started speaking out about it in general conversation. It was amazing how many people I came into contact with who were going through or had been suffering from depression. I began to realise, as people in my life began to ask me questions, of the metaphysical nature, that I had long forgotten about my gifts and abilities that I was born with. I had unknowingly pushed my abilities away, suppressing them deep within. However, the persistent questions of a metaphysical nature began to awaken my psychic medium abilities more and more each day, and I became spiritually stronger, slowly stimulating my abilities back to life.

As my abilities were slowly awakening, I began to realise that Spirit had been pushing me into the direction of service to mankind. Had the universe been teaching me valuable lessons throughout my life? Was it that my life lessons were for the benefit of humanity? Was I to begin my new journey working as a psychic medium, using my gifts and abilities for the betterment of mankind? The questions to myself were constant. In short, the resounding answer was *yes*.

The skills that I had acquired as a frontman and singer-songwriter were applied in my work as a psychic medium. Public speaking comes to mind, as I was asked to perform a presentation at a psychic expo in 2016, which is run annually. Naturally, I was quite at home when it came to taking the stage and speaking to an audience about psychic and mediumistic abilities. Performing live audience readings and answering metaphysical questions, which some of the audience members were puzzled by, where the activities of the day.

The time on stage had ended quite quickly, as my friend Mary, one of the event organisers, gave me a signal to draw my presentation to a close. The time seemed to fly, as I was really getting into my presentation. It felt as though I had just started, as I wanted to continue sharing more of my knowledge. I was so at home on stage, in front of the audience, that I could have kept going for much longer. But the time restrictions were in place. Thanking the audience for their time, I graciously left the stage with a strong knowingness that I could do this type of work for the rest of my life.

One reading that I performed for a young lady at the psychic expo presentation started with a reading that I had performed the day before while reading for another lady at a crystal shop called Krystal Kamali, where I had been reading by this time now for a few years.

In the reading on the previous day, a huge dog appeared from the other side of the veil, sitting there on his haunches with a loving smile, waiting patiently to let his owner know that he was happy in his new home. The client, on the previous day, that I had performed a reading for, owned mostly all the messages that I had brought through from spirit, except for the huge dog, that had my attention, actively making its presence known to me. The spirit of the dog was so strong with me that I knew he wanted me to pass a message to his owner. Since my client couldn't own the dog and with the strength of the dog coming through, I felt the message would somehow be eventually delivered to the rightful recipient.

At the psychic expo the next day, I explained to the audience that as a psychic medium, you know without a doubt the strength of a message when it comes through. In the case of the spirit of the dog, I knew it to be a solid connection with the dog's spirit, having a strong, authentic knowing of the spirit energy. For example, two plus two definitely equals four. You know, without a doubt, when you are getting the right interpretations, messages, and signs. As I began to explain the story of the previous day, a lady in the front row *gasped*. I heard her say, *"That's my dog."* I was floored and proceeded to make sure that it was, in fact, the lady's dog.

As it turns out, the lady's dog actually passed the day before, while I was in another town performing a reading for another client. Instantly, the huge dog came through, as he had done on the previous day. I explained what he looked like to the young lady and that he was sitting on his haunches, lovingly looking on. I love dogs and animals in general, which is possibly, why the young lady's beautiful dog had come through to me.

The lady's grandmother also came through that day, and she showed me how she had passed. This was also validated. The validation of the young lady's grandmother coming through was also a validation for the young lady's dog. Well, that's the short story of that situation, which was absolutely amazing. I had learned something new that day. The way that passed loved ones come through shows that spirit energies can come through in any way that they can; they wish to have your undivided attention and ultimately get their messages across to their loved ones still here on earth.

But the question remains: Had I been asked to do the expo so that I could pass on the message to the young lady that her beautiful dog was okay and very happy and had healed from the cancer that had taken its life? Had I been sent there to tell her that her grandmother was happy and healed on the other side of the veil as well? Without a doubt, I believe that this is what had definitely taken place. There must have been a lot of love in the young lady's family. The grandmother and the beautiful dog very strongly came through to let the young lady know that they were both okay, watching over her and guiding her with pure love.

I thought it necessary to write about my personal journey, to take you on a trip down memory lane to further point out how I see that "life's purpose" begins at birth. Throughout my journey, up until now, I can easily see that Spirit had been calling me for many years while I unintentionally ignored the calling. The bonus is that I learned a lot more by unintentionally not acknowledging my abilities. I didn't understand that I could be out there in the world helping people in the way that I now do. Although I had been associated with many clairvoyants, psychics, and healers over the years, I knew that I was also one of them, while at the same time, I didn't believe that I was one of them.

It's ambiguous, I know. But that's the best way that I can describe my situation. Eventually, Spirit upped the volume, and I had no choice but to listen. I had to own my abilities, and it was all in the divine timing. As I remember that time when I began to raise my awareness from the depths, prompted by endless metaphysical questions by Karen and others, I can now see that Spirit wanted me at that time to begin my spiritual path.

Looking back before my now "structured metaphysical abilities," I had been cornered by the universal divine forces, with no place to go except forward, towards the light, to where I am at today, which is helping people. I am very proud and very honoured to be among many others in this world in the same field, with the same abilities, shining the light over mankind in their own unique ways.

Always follow what resonates within you. That way, you remain true to your authentic self. Once you reach your destination of what you are incarnated here on earth to do and achieve, your life will be restructured, forever changed. As a lightworker, you will attract what you need and the people that you need to help you move forward on your chosen pre-incarnate life's purpose, at precisely the right moment.

CHAPTER 6

BEING AWARE OF YOUR PERSONAL SIGNS AND SYMBOLS

Signs and symbology are the keys to your gateway of life.
Becoming familiar with your personal signs and symbols can
unlock the puzzles that may lie ahead of you.

—*Doc O'Toole*

Being aware of what is around you at any time in your life can be of considerable benefit. Contrary to this, walking through life with the blinders covering your eyes can also be detrimental. At times, we may choose to turn a blind eye to specific events and situations within our lives, but this at the best of times can prove dangerous, and you may find yourself missing out on experiencing vital opportunities. It could also be deemed as a little reckless, like driving a car with your hands off the wheel. Your vehicle drives aimlessly along the highway of life, without any real purpose or direction.

Fear of the unknown is what can cause you to turn a blind eye to life. By not wanting to see what is happening around you, you may be robbing yourself of your personal growth, leaving you stagnant, floating aimlessly throughout the sea of life. We aren't born with a mechanical GPS installed within our human system. We internally write out our life maps as we live our lives step by step, day by day, hour by hour, guided by life lessons from which we have successfully grown. However, we are born with an "intuitive GPS" within us all that we should really listen to more than we actually do.

Being unaware of signs and symbols is totally okay. You will definitely learn what your personal signs and symbols are throughout your travels along the highway of life. Perhaps you aren't any the wiser, being unaware of signs and symbols, and that's totally okay, too. Eventually, you will have inevitably gathered your personal signs and symbols throughout your life experiences. This gathering of information will continue until the day comes for you to leave this lifetime, as you transition into the next.

One straightforward explanation of signs is that when we are born, we don't know that it is dangerous to put your hand in a fire or onto a hot stove. Very quickly though, we will inevitably find out by touching the heated objects or by listening to the guided loving warnings, of our parents, who repeatedly tell us, not to touch the fire or you will be burned, which sometimes we ignore, finding out the hard way.

We are born with five senses, one of which is feeling. In reality, if we get too close to a fire, our feeling radar senses will kick in within a split second, warning us to back off, signalling that this could get very ugly very quickly. This may result in a one-way ticket, travelling in an ambulance, heading full speed to a nearby hospital's burn unit.

So, what we now understand is feelings, which is one of the five senses. Touch is a perception resulting from the activation of neural receptors, generally in the skin, hair follicles, tongue, throat, and mucosa. This is something we all know about. But let's go internal and explore our inner "feelings."

I liken internal feelings to a radar, used for navigation, for example, in submarines. We experience feelings of love, hate, happiness, hunger, thirst, danger, tiredness, and fatigue. If we obey these feelings, they keep us safe and out of the danger zone, health-wise. We should choose to listen to our bodies more often than we actually do.

The internal feelings can also be viewed as a safety net or, on the contrary, used in creative ways, for example, the way an interior designer uses their senses. An interior designer uses their feeling senses to choose colours, furniture, designs, and so forth, to decorate the room she or he is contracted to decorate.

Think about it for a second. Have you walked past a painting or portrait hanging on your lounge room wall, time and time again? Each time that you walk past it, you have that strong feeling that it doesn't feel right to be hanging in its current place, getting the sense that the artwork would feel better displayed in another room. Eventually, after months of procrastination, you move the artwork to that other room that you were prompted to display it in. All of a sudden, with the validation of feeling, you *"feel"* that now the artwork seems very right in its new environment.

You may feel proud that you finally listened to the internal nudging within you to move the piece of artwork, which may also become one of your conversational pieces over that following weeks, as you describe to a friend about the experience you have witnessed in regards to listening to your feelings. You will feel happy and proud that you finally listened to your inner wisdom, along with your inner knowing. Finally, you can now stop walking in and out of that room, staring at the artwork that felt so out of place, as it currently resides now in its rightful place.

With the artwork now hanging in the correct room, you can't help yourself. You walk into this room, staring at the painting on the wall, now noticing how right it *feels*. You may question yourself about this repeatedly while knowing that now the artwork is being displayed in its rightful hanging space. That reason is that the artwork simply *feels* right in its new place.

I began to understand this feeling many years ago when I was contracted to refurbish a beautiful sweeping staircase. I spent a few weeks on the staircase, preparing it for a French polish application. Yes, I could have easily applied polyurethane, but I instead chose to use the technique of French polishing. It seemed more fitting and felt right to apply this type of finish, as this was a substantial, grand home, on ten acres. I applied around one hundred and twenty coats of shellac to the railings of the sweeping staircase, finishing with high-gloss white enamel paint on the closed stringers, the landing, the risers, and the balusters. The staircase then had a natural sisal carpet, which ran up through the centre of the staircase treads. It looked absolutely stunning.

The areas of French polishing reflected depth, with a high shine. I was so proud of the results of the staircase that I couldn't stop looking at it. This puzzled me. Why did everything seem so perfect? What could be wrong? I wondered.

Soon after, a French polisher arrived to quote other sections of this beautiful home. He was amazed at the results that I had achieved with the staircase, offering me a job immediately subcontracting for his company. I questioned the French polisher, asking him, "Why is it that I keep looking at the results of my work on the staircase?"

He explained, "It's human nature to look for faults even when there aren't any. When a job is done to a high-quality finish, such as this staircase, you are simply attracted to it." The French polisher went on to say that you're attracted to the beauty of what has been created.

By feeling what is around you, you can find the right path. In some cases, this will help keep you safe. There have been many reported cases over the years of people walking home after a night out on the town. While walking home, they make a mistake and venture into a part of the town or city that they know nothing about. However, if you are street smart, you will have already learned the signs of a dangerous neighbourhood from your previous experiences. Other people, however, haven't experienced the signs of a dangerous part of the city at night. I have spoken to people in conversation who have experienced this daunting feeling of *"Oh no, this definitely doesn't feel right."* They have acted on their senses, learning and listening to the signs, which led them away from impending danger and into a much safer area.

I know of one lady who experienced a dangerous situation in New York City. Karen had been visiting New York for a week before returning home to Australia. Every day, she would venture out of her hotel room to explore the beautiful city, which she loved so much.

One day, while I was at work in Australia, I received a message from Spirit that Karen was in danger. Straight away, I rang Donald, her partner, asking him if he had heard from his wife at all. Donald is a healthy sceptic, but he listened to what I had to say. He had been very used to me and my psychic abilities by this time, as he had witnessed firsthand both my psychic abilities and my mediumship. Keeping calm and low key, I suggested to Donald to contact his wife to check on her, as I felt something wasn't sitting right with me. He reacted positively and rang Karen in New York City straight away.

As it turned out, Karen had been out on her daily adventures in New York City, dazed by the beauty and the fact that she was in New York. She had wandered aimlessly into a part of the city where you must have your wits about you. By the time that Donald had contacted her, she had made it back to where she considered it to be a safe zone.

After speaking with Donald, Karen rang me from New York straight away, knowing that I knew that she had wandered into an unsafe area. I could hear in her voice that she was frightened and a little shook up, but now safe and calming down, she joked about her experience in her typical manner.

Karen had become confused with the streets and the way that they ran. The grid patterns are a little different from what she was used to here in Australia. The same thing has happened to me while visiting Boston. I was a little bamboozled with some of the street grid patterns as well. Usually, I have a great sense of direction, mapping the streets out in my mind. I came across a postal worker on his rounds and tagged along with him, and he kindly delivered me to my street address, free of charge.

Sensing traffic while driving or riding a motorcycle, for one thing, can be a massive advantage to us all. Being a gearhead, I love muscle cars and motorcycles. While driving along the roadways, on my way to work, or travelling down a freeway, I am always aware of what is around me. Sometimes on a long trip, I'll play a game that I call "guess what this driver is going to do." There is always a chance of some danger while driving. I have fine-tuned my senses to the point where I know when to back off from another vehicle, predicting they will move into another lane to turn off to another road. Sometimes the driver will leave this decision to the very last minute while cutting traffic off in the process.

I have evaded a few incidents throughout my life by remaining consciously aware of my surroundings by tuning in and listening to my senses. Don't get me wrong—there is always that chance of a collision that is totally out of your hands. By sensing what the other driver is thinking about doing next, whether it be a lane change or pulling out in front of you, you can always maintain your sense of alertness, using that intuitive radar within you.

Sometimes, I'm not sure what people are thinking when they decide to pull out on you in traffic. Some clearly see the oncoming traffic, but they still feel the need to pull out in front of you. It's as if they have to be in line at the supermarket checkout first before any other person gets to the registers. Remember that there is always time to achieve what you need to do.

You really don't have to understand why a person shops the way they do or drives a vehicle the way that they do. The point is that you must be aware and read the situations, using your intuitive radar with which you were born with. Doing this will hopefully keep you and those around you safe and out of harm's way.

We commute each day with lots of activity going on around us at any given time, which is a perfect environment to practice and test your senses. However, by fine-tuning your senses in traffic, being aware of your surroundings also fine-tunes your senses for everyday life situations. We all have senses, with some of those senses being stronger than others. However, if we exercise our less dominant senses like we exercise our muscles, they will become stronger while at the same time strengthening our more dominant senses.

I guess you were hoping to read about other types of signs, symbols, and senses. You will, but the above is no less important and works just the same as seeing a feather, a coin, or a ladybug as a symbol or sign. While these are also daily signs for us, I also like to see people safe and sound, enjoying their life and journeys while here on earth. It's not all fun. There are dangers that we face that we must be aware of.

The fact is by explaining what may be perceived as a negative side of what a sign is or what a "senses-alarm" going off internally within you is, I know that you have experienced some sort of situation or the same type of scenarios in your lifetime. Therefore, I understand that you feel and can relate to what I have previously written, I did this purposefully, to get your attention and set in motion how you may interpret and feel a sign, symbol, or being in tune with yourself and your senses.

Now for the Good Stuff

A few years back, on a crisp Sunday morning, I was sitting at the top of a flight of stairs outside my home. The August winds were blowing, as they do here in the Southern Highlands each year. I was surrounded by a well-established garden area. I would sit at the top of the stairs each morning for my morning ritual meditation. On this day, I mentioned that it was quite windy, with the trade winds blowing. I saw a white feather floating towards me. The feather was not being controlled by the wind and looked as though someone or something had a hold of it, managing its every movement while in flight.

Instantly, I heard a voice in my mind say that the feather was my "guardian angel." I knew and felt this to be true. In front of me, where I sat at the top of the stairs, was an alleyway that ran along the rear of my home. The alley was about twenty feet in length. Sitting there as the white feather flew around behind me, from left to right, making its way to be in front of me, I then made a request to the white feather to test it out. I felt kind of silly trying to prove what I already knew to be true, but I thought it would be fun just the same.

As the white feather flew mostly straight as an arrow in the wind, from behind me to in front of me, I requested that it go to the end of the alleyway. I was amazed when it did. I then asked for the feather to come back to me. And again, the feather responded to my request. There was a window sill to the right of me, so I decided to push my luck a little further and requested the feather, on its way back to me, to sit on the window sill. By this time, I was covered in confirmation chills as the feather, as you may have already guessed, sat on the sill.

We all have angels, spirit guides, and passed loved ones around us, throughout our lives. At the time of the white feather incident, I had been going through a transition in my life. This miracle or serendipity of my guardian angel, making its presence gave me strength and encouragement that the divine was with me and that all would be okay in its own divine time.

As I wrote the word "guardian angel" here in my quiet space, the light above me flickered a few times softly. To me, this indicates that my guardian angel is with me as I write about the feather incident. A flickering light can indicate that a lightbulb is on the way out or that any number of things can be happening. But not this time. This time, it was synchronicity. I could feel it, and I know it to be a message of validation from my guardian angel.

I have had many experiences with feathers. Such as through the rainy and windy winters of winter here in the Southern Highlands. I had my desk up against my office wall facing under the window, facing out, looking onto a very green shrub area.

A few months before this, I had lost a great friend, Ronnie, who I believe had the heart of an angel. She would do things for people in silence, totally unconditionally. You would not hear her talk about what she may have done for someone in need of assistance. It was who she was, and I admired that integrity in her greatly. Being a musician, I wrote and recorded a song dedicated to Ronnie, called "Angel in the Sky," to keep her memory alive. I then gave copies of this song to her family members and close friends, which they obviously loved and cherished.

Sitting at my desk that winter while trying to keep warm, I noticed a white feather resting on a leaf amongst the shrubs. I felt this to be a sign from Ronnie, that she was with me and she was well and free of cancer, sending her love. Weeks went by, bringing the winter winds, snow, and torrential rains, which were weeks long, but still, that little white feather that I had seen many weeks before sat on the leaf outside my window. I would look out the window every morning and evening, and to my amazement, the white feather was always there. It was still on the shrubs leaf many months later, and it was still there on the day that I moved out.

Ronnie's passing had been a shock to me. I called her one night to see how she was since we hadn't been in contact for a long while. She told me that she was unwell. I had to pry it out of her to see what the matter was. Ronnie eventually said to me that she had been diagnosed with stage-four cancer. I was totally shocked! That's not what I was expecting to hear at all.

She survived four months after that conversation. I made it a point to call her regularly, offering her comfort and support. She was so brave, with minimal complaints, while she set about experiencing things in life that she had never done. I guess It was her bucket list. To my amazement, she told me that she had never been to an arena concert. Well, she did that; she went with her girlfriend to see her favourite band, Bon Jovi.

One night, I awoke suddenly at 2:30 a.m. as if I had been woken up. Climbing out of bed, I walked into my lounge room, where I could feel that someone was trying to get my attention. As I sat on the lounge, I felt the strong urge to log on to my Facebook account. As soon as I logged on, I saw in the feed that Ronnie had passed away.

After Ronnie's passing, she was still posting comments on her Facebook page. There were pictures of guitars that I liked and other messages for other friends. I did make some phone calls, however, gingerly asking if anyone had been posting on her Facebook page, but the only person to have her login details was Ronnie herself. So I guess that she was still logging on leaving her friends and family messages and signs that she was now out of pain and very happy on the other side of the veil.

I have heard of people posting on their Facebook pages after they have left this world, but I never truly believed it. I was a sceptic of this until I witnessed it for myself.

I have since found out that Spirit energy can manipulate electro-magnetic energy, such as making your lights flicker because spirit is energy. But as mentioned before, check your light bulb to see if it needs changing before jumping to any conclusions. You will know what is actually going on through learning, understanding, and evolving with your own intuition and the magical spiritual experiences of this world.

Spirit for Dinner

Donald is what you would call "a healthy sceptic." He is very supportive of my gifts and abilities, sometimes turning a blind eye while calmly retreating to another room or changing the subject to talk about the news or something of interest that took his fancy on that day any time a metaphysical happening arises.

One night over dinner, with Donald and Karen, while sitting at the well-laid-out table, quietly eating away, I suddenly felt a Spirit energy run their finger horizontally across the middle of my back. You know the feeling: your back muscles retract when that spot has pressure applied. Even though I knew what it was, I still turned around to see *who* it was, to find no one standing there. I didn't think anyone was watching, so I continued to eat my dinner. The next occurrence took me by surprise. If you know me well, you would see that I zone out into my world, especially while eating. Next, I heard Karen saying to Donald, "You can't say you never saw that?" In defence, Donald replied with wide-open eyes, "How could I not? I was staring at Doc when it happened." Karen and I found this very amusing. I sat there thinking while having a laugh to myself, "How cool was that?" without even realising an audience had been looking on.

The look on Donald's face was priceless. It was as though he actually saw the spirit, who was kindly letting me know that she was there. I say "she" because I felt it was female energy. I had seen an elderly lady there weeks before, standing outside a door in the hallway. She was a tall, thin woman about eighty years old. We found out later that an elderly lady of a similar description had lived at this home years before. The spirit energy was just letting me know that she was around.

Spirit energies use what you are familiar with to get your attention. They use what you know and what you are used to within your daily life to get their messages across. When interpreting the messages sent from spirit, you must become used to your own signs and symbols to understand when they want your attention so they can then communicate their messages, through you to their loved ones here on this earthly plane. I love how time and time again, spirit energies use my sense of humour to get their messages across. At times, it's like laughing in church. I can't help but laugh out loud as spirit energies entice my humour.

Cloud Messages

Signs and symbols, as mentioned throughout this book, are everywhere. They are all around us. The problem is that we don't recognise them due to our busy day-to-day schedules we must fulfil, such deadlines, work commitments, weekly shopping, or all of the above at the same time. We think that we are always too busy to stop and feel the cosmos and to take time out to "sit in the silence."

Making time to have time for you each day is necessary. You may only have a window of five to ten minutes to do this, but don't worry if that's all the time that you have. At least you have made time for yourself. We all know about the "power nap," don't we? A power nap can feel like you have slept for hours, and yet it is only a fifteen-minute siesta.

Taking time out from your daily grind has the same sensational feeling as a power nap. Sitting in a meditative position, either in the garden or a particular room in your home or office, or sometimes in your parked car, and zoning out, allows messages from the divine to come through to you. Have you ever done this to find that, suddenly, the answer to a problem you have been dealing with comes through with crystal clarification?

We must learn to make room for signs and symbols in our lives so we may take full advantage of what our passed loved ones, angels, and spirit guides are trying to communicate to us. Signs and symbols are also used in everyday decision-making to help you gauge what to do with a particular type of situation as you decide the best avenue to take.

Not that long ago, I had been working very hard in my job to fulfil a painting contract in time for my clients so they could put their rental property back on the market. I had been pushing myself to the limit— and a little beyond that, as well. However, I still had time for my daily morning meditation, as tired and as worn out as I was. At the end of the day, I would arrive home, change into comfortable clothing, and walk barefoot out on the lawn. This is highly recommended! I can feel the tingling energies from the grassy earth beneath the souls of my feet, grounding me and restoring my energies from a hard day's work. It is very therapeutic.

This one day, as I arrived home from work, my body had been aching from many weeks of working too hard. Instead of walking the beautiful green lawn, as I usually did, I decided this day to lie down on the lawn, flat on my back, looking up at the blue summer sky. I could feel the earth tingling throughout my body, which is a fantastic feeling. As I felt the pain in my body begin to relax, I started to zone out as I stared up at the puffy white clouds high above me. This was nothing new to me, as I had been doing this throughout my life. This is a way that you can see the world from a different perspective. There is something very magical about it.

While staring up at the blue summer sky, watching the clouds, I noticed that one particular cloud was in the shape of a large, detailed horse head. It reminded me of the stallion on a property where I lived many years before. My sister, Vickie, who passed away many years ago, loved horses very much. She would draw horses and ride horses, and she always wanted one. Everything was horse-related with her.

As my mind drifted off while lying on the earth that day, a memory of the wristwatch that our grandmother had gifted my sister came to mind. I still have that watch in the original case in which it arrived. I often go on these mind-mapping "thought journeys," never knowing what will come through. However, on this day, it was a beautiful message from above. After resting for a few hours from a day of not painting but rather performing as a psychic medium, I received a message stating that our grandmother had passed away, at the ripe old age of ninety-four.

My mind quickly flashed back and ran through the cloud message that I had just received. On quick reflection, I soon realised that the cloud had been a message, informing me that our grandmother had passed away.

CHAPTER 7
SHAKE YOUR FOUNDATIONS

From a rock 'n roll singer/songwriter to a psychic medium.

When Spirit was ready for me to step up to own my gifts and abilities, I felt the earth move, feeling the tectonic activation, definitely moving me in a new direction of purpose. I learned quickly that Spirit will definitely let you know when you are to start using your talents for the betterment of mankind, by shaking your foundations to the very core— "shaken, but not stirred." Well, maybe a little stirred. I likened myself to a rug, having all of the dust shaken vigorously from my rug of life.

With the dust then landing, settling with a new perspective, a new purpose, and direction in life, becoming activated to, "get up and get busy," by using my abilities that I was born with to help people of this world, in a newer way, more structured way than I had done previously. In turn, becoming active to illuminate the path and journey of mankind so that mankind can commit to keeping the perpetual healing, paying forward.

To me, this was a new direction, from out of left-field, from the familiar ground that I had been so familiar with over the many previous years. This new way for me was one that I never thought possible. It never entered my mind that I was a psychic medium. I had up to this time used my abilities, unlabelled and unstructured, for the better part of my life, never stopping to look at how it was even possible that I was also capable of psychic abilities. The medium side of me was, I believe, a bonus.

I didn't have a clue what was happening to me or what was happening to the familiar world that I had been so comfortably accustomed to, in which I had resided in for many years. I had been a rock 'n roll frontman, a singer-songwriter, for thirty years. I had been a member of many bands, always working on my vocal abilities, giving 100 percent and more to each and every new project, always with the unwavering belief that I would fulfil my lifelong dream to be a successful musician. I gave all that I had to succeed in my chosen career, and then some. I had sacrificed a comfortable way of living as we know it, stepping outside my comfort zone to follow my passion, my hopes and dreams, with a passionately burning fire, intensely ignited within me, running hot for many years. Along with this, I had a burning desire to become the best rock vocalist that I could possibly be while always pushing myself to the limit.

For years, I honed and moulded my craft, overcoming my weaknesses and operating vibrantly with my strengths as a singer-songwriter vocalist, producer, and guitarist. When that wasn't enough, I entered the conservatorium of music on a casual basis to study the saxophone. Being a musician, for me, was a hard life and a struggle at times, but I loved it.

I had experienced living on the breadline, living where I could and having very little money, but I never lost the faith that I would make it to the world stage. I would take any job offered to me to survive. I worked as a roadie, an embroiderer, a chef, a driver, a labourer on job sites, and the list goes on. All the while, I never lost faith, always believing in myself and in my abilities. That one night on stage, with my band, made every bit of the struggle that I endured every bit of blood sweat and tears, well worth it. No matter how big or small the gig was, I loved the art of being a musician. Rock 'n roll had been my way of life.

I had always loved the haunting, spiritual sounds that whaled from a saxophone. I just laughed out loud, because as I sit here writing out how the saxophone gets me deep in my soul and makes me feel spiritually, with a magical feeling not of this world, how it penetrates my soul to the core, enticing past life memories that I just can't recall but know existed, that famous song "Baker Street" began to play in the background. "Baker Street," if you are unfamiliar with, is a 1978 hit by Gerry Rafferty that has an *amazing* saxophone solo throughout it. For me, "Baker Street," or the song "Saturday Night" by the Australian band Cold Chisel, along with a host of other jazz and blues numbers are the ultimate songs for me to learn on the saxophone. I did actually learn "Saturday Night" on the sax a few years back. Wow, it's just an amazing soulful tune to perform. You just feel the urge to want to play it over and over again. I have always connected with soul-deep songs. I connect deeply and can never get enough of the history and the sound of blues and soul music. *I get it.*

Looking back now, I can see that my abilities as a seer had always been with me, playing a significant part in my songwriting and stage performance. However, through the early years of my life, I also believed that everyone was the same. That is until my friends and associates started giving me that silent sideways looks, in jest. Yes, I was the different one, the odd one out, the sensitive one. But I also loved being that person. I wasn't the same as everyone else, and I knew it. I was definitely an individual. When I speak with some friends and associates these days who have known me for many years, as I now explain to them that I currently work as a psychic medium, they are not at all surprised. Actually, I'm more surprised by their responses. It seems I was the last one to find out.

As I mentioned in chapter 5, I believe that when we are born, so too is our life's purpose. We aren't familiar with, nor do we understand, what our life's purpose is or, in most cases, that a life's purpose even exists for each and every one of us. But eventually, later on in life, our life's purpose does become a reality, whether we are looking for it or not.

Some people are very fortunate that they are living their life's purpose from a very young age. With others, it takes much longer and begins much later in life. This, to me, is self-explanatory, as we are all vibrating on different levels. When you are ready, Spirit will let you know. With the belief that we have all lived in a previous lifetime indicates that we are most definitely, all on different levels, some more advanced than others. This means some of us are to learn more life lessons before we begin the work that we were born to.

Working for Spirit is the best job in the world. I just love that I was chosen to do this job. It never ceases to amaze me how Spirit orchestrates situations and events for me to be at a particular place, to pass a message on to somebody in need, delivering a message from their passed loved ones from the other side of the veil.

Spirit orchestrations happen to me frequently. When this first started happening, I would go to the place where I was instructed to go to. I would, for example, walk into a store that I felt that I was being directed to. I'd be looking around for something to buy, all the while wondering how in the world I was going to know who to talk to. Furthermore, I'd be thinking that this was crazy. I would think to myself, *Am I just making this up?* Before I knew it, without intruding, I would be talking to someone who needed the message from their loved one. Sometimes, for the recipient, it was absolutely perfect timing. I would walk away from the store with a new product in hand, absolutely gobsmacked at what had just taken place, knowing that I had just made someone's day that much better.

After a few occasions of what I call "orchestrated meetings" or "driveway readings," I began to become used to and trust the instructions from Spirit. At other times, I would be instructed to go to the hardware store or attend to some everyday errands, and I would come into contact with someone needing guidance. However, when I think back on the string of events that led me to the person who needed help, I see clearly that I had been directed to be at a particular place at a specific time to pass on the message.

It's just amazing! Spirit never sleeps, always directing human traffic to their next destination. We are continually learning, forever evolving, forever growing. This will always be. I embrace it all wholeheartedly.

For the past two weeks, during April 2018, I had returned to the USA to attend John Holland's Advanced Masterclass Mediumship workshop for the second year running. For your information, I am presently sitting on a plane flying back from the States as I write this chapter. So forgive me if it sounds a little flighty.

My USA trips usually are spiritually eventful. When I fly from Sydney to attend one of these spiritual events in the USA, it is a long trip to travel, as you can well imagine. The flights are usually around twenty-three hours, but the travel time works out to be about thirty hours in total. This doesn't bother me at all. Yes, I can hear you gasp as you read this, thinking, *Wow, that's a long way to go for a weekend course*. I have heard all this before. Indeed, to me, it isn't about how far I have to go. I look at how far I have come. It's always a journey, never a destination.

Working for Spirit is a journey, I never think about how far I have to go until I reach a destination. That doesn't even enter my mind. The fact that I can help mankind, along with the passion and excitement vibrating within me, is all that I need to know. I keep travelling forward, always moving, one step at a time, one foot in front of the other, without thinking, *Are we there yet?* What is that anyway, "Are we there yet"? If you think about it, we are always there, wherever we are, at any given time.

I'm continually learning, studying and growing with my psychic and mediumistic abilities, growing forward each and every day to become the best I can be, using my gifts and abilities to help the people of this world. I believe that there is never truly a final destination. If you start thinking in this way, then it is time to branch out, to find what really excites you. Find what it is that is invigorating to you because there you will discover your true passion and your calling.

When we are passionate about what we are doing, there is never a final destination. We are on a continuous, evolving journey. A destination to me is a full-stop. I believe the final destination that we perceive during our lifetime evolves into a higher understanding within the afterlife, which we eventually return to. Remember, we are here on this earthly plane to develop, grow, and learn. This, in turn, will give you the knowledge needed to help mankind, by spreading awareness, light, and love among our fellow humans so that they too learn and evolve to a higher level of consciousness. This is when the newly enlightened will grow to the next level of their journey while sharing their enlightenment with others so they will also expand to their next level, carrying the flame of knowledge even further to light up the lives around them, illuminating the path forward. I call this perpetual healing. ("Perpetual evolution" is another appropriate description.)

I do believe that we do incarnate more than once, each time growing to a higher level of consciousness. That higher level that we reach is due to the life lessons we have learned in previous lifetimes and within this lifetime, thus transporting with us all the accumulated knowledge from our own experiences and from our previous incarnation, spreading the love, light, and wisdom among mankind, so we grow to a higher understanding with our gifts and abilities we are born with. To me, this is what life is all about. Every material thing that we possess and want is a by-product of our very own existence.

CHAPTER 8

GET UP AND GET BUSY

When you have succeeded, you have success. All it will cost
you is passion, focus, and determination.

—*Doc O'Toole*

As mentioned in a previous chapter, it can take half a lifetime to begin what you were born to do while you inhabit this earthly plane of existence. You may have the skills and abilities for a whole lot of ventures along with the talent and knowledge of doing whatever it is you wish to undertake and do it exceptionally well. You may start out in life as a carpenter, pilot, or lawyer, having an undying passion for your chosen career. All the while, though, throughout your professional years, you may also feel that something is missing within your life, something you just can't put the finger on. You will feel, with strong knowledge and a strong knowing, that there is a greater something out there that you should be undertaking. At the same time, you may also confuse that feeling by believing you will be highly successful in your chosen profession. While that may be true, you may also still feel that there is something not quite right, that something is missing within your life.

However, you may also be successful in your chosen career, finding that you work hard for it every step of the way. In some ways, it may seem like a battle, the road of resistance, you might say. You come to understand that while you are struggling and finding it hard to achieve, taking one step forward and two steps back, while your peers and other associates in a similar field seem to lead a blessed life, turning everything they touch to gold. This, by the way, is totally fine.

Time and time again, you ask yourself, *How do they do it so easily? What do they know that I don't know?* Frustratingly, you know that you have the skills, gifts, and talents to be at the top of your game in your chosen career, but it's just not working for you. However, you persist anyway, having total faith and belief in oneself.

I know that one of the secrets to finding your life's purpose is to run your own race, to get out of the passenger seat and grab hold of the steering wheel of life. Become a leader instead of a follower, and never dumb yourself down. Stand on your own two feet and dare to be you. Have the courage to step outside your comfort zone, venturing through the doorway into success. Be totally, humbly you.

If you look at a young child, they are all this and more. Remember, you, at one time in your life, were a young child who ran your own race, who wasn't afraid to step outside your comfort zone. You didn't even know that the phrase "comfort zone" even existed at that young age. Nothing would stop you from moving forward as a young child. You had no boundaries, no fear, and definitely no "yeah, but" in your vocabulary. You just went for it.

So what happens?

The expectations of others for one. Trying to please people for another. These two examples are among many explanations. Society's beliefs, rules, and regulations were a part of our training ground as we grew into adulthood. I'm not saying we don't need rules and regulations; we most certainly do. What I'm saying is to take control of your life, to slide across from the passenger seat in your vehicle of life to take control of your steering wheel, therefore taking total control of your destination. Remember that what works for another does not mean it will work for you. We are all uniquely individual.

Nevertheless, do not be too hard on yourself. In everything and every situation, we learn, grow, and evolve to build our internal tools for when the universe needs us to begin our work, launching us into full swing with whatever our life's purpose is to be.

As I became aware that I was genuinely psychic and then understanding, that a medium wasn't necessarily the size of a shirt one would purchase, instead, it pertained to the ability to communicate with spirit energy, I began learning about my gift. I dived into the deep end to start understanding my abilities from an array of sources, such as books, the Internet, and from others who had worked as a psychic and medium for many years. I began travelling to the USA to attend John Holland's workshops. I also participated in psychic and mediumship workshops here in Australia, as well. In the back of my thoughts, I intend to travel to the Arthur Findlay College in England at some point soon to further my education as a medium.

I have now, at this point in my life, "owned" my abilities for the past five years. In essence, I have put learning and understanding my abilities into top gear.

Eventually, I answered my calling, while at the same time discovering that close friends already knew what I was capable of. As my longtime friend Tracy, or TJ, as I call her, said during a phone conversation recently, *You use to freak me out with what you would come out with.* TJ use to hope that when she came over for a visit for a Saturday night movie hang out, that I wouldn't say anything that wasn't of general conversation. As I explained to her, I had no idea what was actually happening. I didn't realise how unnatural my conversations were with her or others for that matter. Nor did I understand that I was freaking her out—it was all normal to me. These days, TJ laughs about those early days and is quite proud of the journey that I am on.

Now I am working as a psychic medium more professionally. I am now structured and don't unknowingly freak people out. That's the last thing I want to do to anyone, unless, of course, my wonky sense of humour lights up, as it sometimes does.

By learning and studying—reading books, watching and attending platforms and seminars, watching DVDs from well-known mediums, and attending mediumship workshops by John Holland in the United States and other mediums here in Australia, I now have a more professional approach when delivering a message to someone. However, there is always room for improvement, which you inevitably learn along the way. You will always be massaging and refining your presentation and the delivery of your craft within your chosen field for the rest of your life.

"Get up and get busy" is a phrase I recently coined. The statement illustrates what one must do to take the next step, now and beyond, to succeed in a particular area of life. Please always remind yourself, "one step at a time." You can't learn everything in a week and expect to go out into the world as a professional. It takes time, just like any recipe does. You can't buy a chocolate cake mix, open up the packet, and expect the cake to magically jump out on to your fine china plate. You must follow the instructions on the package to achieve the desired outcome. We must savour every step, every lesson, and every new piece of information to be the best that we can be in our chosen fields.

Yes, it does require a lot of patience with your passion. More importantly, it requires becoming humble and growing within your own space and time while dealing with and understanding the workings of the ego.

In the beginning, it is easy to stay focused. However, as you transition forward, you will find that life will always test you, periodically interrupting your growth process. Always remember that everything is as it should be. Situations will inevitably crop up, taking you away from the goals that you have laid out for yourself. That's totally okay, though. Just remember to get back on track at the opportune time.

There is no time except divine time, so don't become discouraged if you are interrupted. Just go with the flow. As you see your goals through to the end, you will become successful, one step at a time. Each step is always about the journey, not the destination.

Writing this book was very easy in the beginning. Then the challenges started kicking in. Such interruptions included my day job, that daily work that brings in the finances to keep the household going. For you, it might pertain to family matters or health issues that call for your divine attention. To you, this is slowing things down. To me, it's helping my book to breathe as it writes itself. These are life's tests, edging you to push through to the next level.

For example, I'm presently staying at a beach-side apartment with a fantastic view of the ocean outside, looking through a set of glazed double sliding doors, with a panoramic view of the outside world, while

Mother Ocean is pounding the shoreline. For the past week, the surf has been flat, which makes it difficult for the keen surfer to catch a wave and have fun riding their surfboards on the back of Mother Nature. Today, however, there is a 3-meter swell rushing to the shoreline. One by one, throughout the day, surfers are showing up in their vehicles, waxing their boards in the grounds of the nearby car park, eager to hit the beach to catch that perfect wave that Mother Nature is providing. It is a Monday, and now, after 4:00 p.m., having completed their daily work tasks, while all throughout their day, the surfers have been thinking of the perfect surf that they will enjoy this afternoon, riding that perfect wave to the shore.

The seed was planted earlier that day, and a manifestation took place within the surfer's minds, forming a belief pattern and therefore creating reality. Two days beforehand, the surf had been flat. Today, however, the surfers take full advantage of the situation, as the waves are in their favour. Therefore, they can enjoy their passion for surfing that perfect wave. As always, the divine timing came right on cue. It never disappoints.

When getting up and getting busy, it may take a little while to achieve what you set out to do, such as the keen surfer waiting for that perfect wave. The surfers know wholeheartedly that the perfect wave will arrive at the divine moment. Patience is the keyword in life as you place your trust in the universe as the divine energies orchestrate the perfect time for you to move forward on an idea or a project. It even tells you when it's time to head off to an appointment to catch that perfect wave.

What you don't want to do is quit before you begin. Just because situations aren't happening in your perfectly thought-out time doesn't mean that you are wasting your time. We cannot control everything the way we think we can. Always remember that if you, for example, come up with an idea for a business, ask yourself, "Where did this idea come from?" I know full well that when it does happen to you when the idea for business makes its presence known within you, it will have arrived from a higher source, which is known to many as a "download."

Where does this download come from, you might ask? Well, if you don't already know, you too have spirit guides around you that were assigned to you before you entered this world. We also have our loved ones and angels around us. All we have to do is listen to the downloads and the promptings of our guides, passed loved ones, and angels, and then trust and have faith. It is always a great idea to ask for validations in the form of a sign to see if you are interpreting the downloaded messages correctly. Signs may not appear straight away. It may take a day, a week, or even a month for the signs to reveal themselves. I have found that if you are not listening to or noticing the signs, the divine energies will persist until you "get it."

As a medium, I ask for validations to confirm the messages that I am to pass on to a client. Most recently, while performing a reading for my client Petra, her grandmother came through with a message. Petra had been waiting ten years to hear from her grandmother, always wanting to know that she had transitioned to the other side, that her grandmother was okay. My client was so delighted, as she had given up hope of ever contacting her beloved grandmother.

As I passed on messages to Petra, a strange message came through from her grandmother. The message was just one word: cabbage. I saw Petra's grandmother standing in her kitchen, preparing a meal. At the same time, I heard the term "cabbage" repeated over and over. I found this strange, but I trusted myself and passed on the message.

I told Petra that I could see her grandmother in her kitchen cooking. I said, "This is a little strange. Your grandmother is repeating the word 'cabbage' over and over. Does this mean anything to you?"

Little did I know that Petra's grandmother always cooked with cabbage in all types of recipes. By the surprised look and joy on Petra's face, it was evident that this message I had downloaded to pass on to my client was very significant. In my mind, I was asking the grandmother energy, "What do you mean, 'cabbage'?" She just repeated the word "cabbage" over and over until I passed on the message.

The delighted look on Petra's face with that one repeated word, along with other messages I delivered, was validation enough that I had seen and heard the right messages and that it was, in fact, Petra's European grandmother whom I was connected to. Petra relayed the message regarding the repeated word, "cabbage," to her husband, Mike, later that evening, who further validated the message.

Mike had been a sceptic and didn't really believe in mediumship until the day he came to support his wife during her first reading with me. He sat there with pen in hand and took copious notes throughout the reading. Mike told me after the reading that he was now a believer, explaining there was no way I could have known the information that came through. Until now, he had not believed in communication with the other side.

Mike and Petra's family had had a recent tragedy in their lives with the passing of someone very dear to them. The young woman came through very strong and clear, with messages to pass on to Petra and Mike. The messages were on point within the family, right down to a particular red dress that the young woman was wearing, which turned out to be their son's favourite photo of the young lady. I was amazed at the strength and connection with this young soul. She had everything in order of what she wanted to say, hitting key points that only those close to her would know and understand. It was as if she knew exactly what messages to pass on to those left behind for healing and transformation. All I can say is that the young soul felt very in tune spiritually and cared an awful lot about her loved ones still living here on earth.

So you see, it's okay to ask and question the messages and feelings that you are receiving from spirit. I would suggest making it a habit to ask for validation. Ask the divine energy for a definitive sign of validation. This could take days or weeks, or you may be delivered a sign very much straight away.

Signs can come in the form of words from a song as you turn on the car stereo or a chance meeting with someone you do not know; it could be a street sign or an overheard conversation in a store, coffee shop, or restaurant. There are many different ways of receiving signs. You just have to put it into practice the art of learning and understanding what a validated sign is for you. I'd suggest starting your own personal journal. Make a list of signs and symbols that resonate with yourself. By doing this regularly, you will soon learn to understand personally how you work and how signs and symbols resonate with you. Remember that what may work for you may not work for others.

When you need help, validation, or understanding of a situation, become used to *"asking"* your guides, angels, or even your passed loved ones for help, as you must ask before they can help you. This is because we are born with free will. Your guides respectfully choose not to interfere until you ask for their help. Don't think, *Oh, they might be too busy. I won't disturb them.* They are always ready and willing to be of assistance to you at all times, as they are omnipresent.

In other ways, I know that your loved ones are always trying to get your attention by sending you signs or a voice in your thoughts for your own personal guidance throughout your life. Now that you understand this, you can start to fine-tune how you receive your messages and signs. The best way to do this is to begin the art of daily meditation.

Meditation is a part of getting up and getting busy. We live in a fast-paced world of computers, deadlines, and expectations. We must not forget our daily work, which feeds our families and pays the rent or mortgage, the utilities, and for the clothes, we wear. The art of meditation will help you stay focused and on track with yourself and with your set goals as you navigate through life.

With your mind quiet and in a relaxed state, while meditating, you will hear and see messages that help navigate you throughout your lifetime. As you practice the art of meditation, you will begin to understand the workings of yourself and the ways that you operate. You will start to understand that which makes you tick. The "wow" factor will become a part of your vocabulary as you are continually amazed at how meditation transforms your life from the constant hustle and bustle to a life of serenity, which you otherwise didn't think possible. You will begin to see the world in a totally new way—more liberated, less judgemental.

Although it's straightforward, meditation is a practice thing.

I have had people and clients say to me, "I can't meditate."

I say, "Have you ever sat on the beach, staring out into the deep blue ocean on a warm summer day?"

They usually say, "Yes, I have."

I reply, "Well, that's a form of meditation. Meditation is the art of nothingness. This means you are sitting in the silence without thought while listening to the silence and its surroundings."

A Simple Meditation

Sit in a quiet space within your home. Sit in a comfortable chair, wearing comfortable, unrestrictive clothes. Close your eyes and begin to breathe, breathing in through your nose and then out through your mouth. Notice that your mind and body begin to relax. After a while of practicing meditation, you will notice a feeling of peace and serenity. This feeling will become addictive. Give yourself ten to fifteen minutes each day to meditate. This is what I call your "Seat-belt to life", which is something you put on before you venture out to begin your day within the world.

That's all there is to meditation. When thoughts rush into your mind, such as, *oh, I must hang the washing out,* or *I must pay that bill,* just let these thoughts come in and let them go out. Don't hang onto these thoughts. Let them go and bring yourself back to the centre of your meditation. With time, your daily meditation practices will become second nature. I would recommend at least fifteen minutes of meditation per day, but don't be concerned if you can't achieve this. If you are running late, I would recommend a five-minute meditation before you head out of your front door by sitting in the silence or find quiet time during your day to meditate.

Sometimes, if I haven't had the time to meditate before heading out for the day, such as on those days that I repeatedly hit the snooze button, I will find a quiet time throughout the day somewhere to sit in the silence. It doesn't really matter what time of the day you choose to meditate, as long as you do it. For you, it may be more convenient to meditate at the end of the day, before you head off to sleep, especially if you have family or work commitments, which is a full-time job within itself. That time of the day could be known as "me time."

Getting up and getting busy is a way of taking control of your life instead of just existing. Over the years, I have heard of people saying they are doing just that. We are all born with unique gifts, no matter how big or small. The gifts you are born with are all very important, no matter how big or small.

To understand what your gifts and abilities are, ask yourself, "What drives me? What really excites me? What are my passions in life?" With questions like these, you will surely find the answer within. If you don't receive an answer straight away, head towards the art of meditation, and the answers will come to you. Also, ask your guides and angels to help you to find the answers.

Honour your gifts and abilities and believe that, yes, you do matter and that, yes, you can make a positive difference in the world, no matter who you are or where you are from. You don't need to justify yourself to anyone.

CHAPTER 9

ONE STEP AT A TIME

Instead of being overwhelmed or underwhelmed, try being "whelmed," which is, to just be?

—Doc O'Toole

It is very easy to become excited and overwhelmed, to want to cross the finish line when you have discovered something new in your life that lights up your exciting passions within you.

You become overjoyed with the new idea of a business venture or a project of learning and discovery. It's very human to want to share your idea with the world. Suddenly you feel on top of your game, with a new lease of happiness and joy, filling your body, mind, and soul.

This type of exhilarating joy happens daily across the world. Uncontrollably, your newfound ideas are then shared verbally or through social media before you have even begun to bring your idea to reality, possibly letting onlookers take full advantage of your thoughts that were downloaded specifically to you. It's a sad fact, but this can and does happen more often than you realise. It is always a wise decision to acknowledge the project that is downloaded, especially to yourself, while keeping it largely quiet as you move into the direction of the new venture, bringing your new business idea or project into fruition while being mindful of moving ahead at a steady pace, at one-step at a time.

I have mentioned the word "download" throughout this book numerous times, while at the same time questioning you, asking, "Where did that thought or download arrive from?" I can explain the concept of download best by stating that it does not come from you but rather through you, from a higher source. I have always known this distinction between the two, but I never really looked at it thoroughly until I began to attend workshops in Australia and in the United States, to learn and understand more about the workings of the mediumship journey that I am experiencing.

Following your own positive instincts is mostly always recommended. However, at times, you can be unsure whether to take these steps or not, which at times can become a little confusing. So, what should you do in these types of situations? First, seek the advice of a trusted friend or colleague whom you look up to and whom you can trust. It's always a good practice to bounce ideas off another person to gain a clearer perspective of your situation, possibly revealing aspects you never considered. Another way would be to ask your guides and angels for a definite sign, showing which direction to head. However, ultimately, it's you that makes the final decision of what to do or where to go. Listen to your body and the messages it is sending you. We were created with an onboard intuitive GPS system, which, unfortunately, most of the time we ignore.

Fear, along with the lack of self-worth, usually stops you from marching forward with your goals, ventures, and ideas. We all go through this at one level or another, and for the most part, we end up learning the hard way. This is not a bad thing as long as you learn as you grow through life. Ultimately this is what creates our personal wisdom and our unique character. Push through the barriers of fears and blockages by literally breathing through the negativities within your life. What's the worst that can happen? Likely, success will be the ultimate outcome.

I was reading for a lovely client recently, whom I will call Pam. She was going through just this type of situation. Pam, who comes from a loving and supportive family, had been struggling with self-worth. She wanted to start her own business, but she was afraid of failure. Pam had mentioned her business ideas to a close friend on a few occasions. She had said to her friend of how she would like to open a beautician shop, which made a lot of sense to me, as she loved to be of service to others and at the time, was working as a volunteer, looking after an elderly woman as her carer. I just love to hear the stories of people looking after the elderly.

While listening to Pam and her situation, which was obviously bothering her, I could clearly feel and see her passion for her family and friends. Being there at a moment's notice, lending a hand or a kind ear when needed, is what she is all about. Pam has always been this way and loved to be there in support of her friends and family, as she had always done. I explained to Pam that she was clearly living a blessed life, always selflessly giving out her help and support needed by her friends and family.

I went on to explain to her that it was also now time for her, that it was okay for her to receive as well as to give. Tears welled up in Pam's eyes as I explained what I could see within her life. It was now time for Pam to start being kind to herself and that it wasn't selfish to give to herself every now and then; she too was worthy, as is everyone.

I have explained that giving and receiving are not two separate energies. In fact, it is one energy. Giving all the time puts one's energy scales out of balance, and this, for Pam, needed to be put back into perspective, back into balance. I went on to explain that if you look at a AA battery, it has a positive at one end and a negative at the opposite end. However, the battery is only one unit and one energy, not two separate energies, and the positive energy will not work without the negative energy. Both energies are capsulated in one cylinder to work as it is intended.

For a battery to work as expected, it must be in balance. I have found, both personally and from an objective point of view, that this is exactly how our lives are intended to operate. If we only continue to give, we end up using all our energies. Then, from there, we reach into our reserve bank of energy until it is depleted. What usually happens from here is that we burn out, leaving us feeling very down and unhappily drained. The person that you may have helped to get up and get going again ends up totally feeling invigorated and full of energy—your energy! So, it would be wise to give a little energy out to help someone and to let them think, understand, learn, and grow, one step at a time while keeping a percentage of your energy for yourself.

We all love to be of service to others, but draining all your energies is not a wise thing to do. It is okay to help someone in their time of need, but it is not okay to go as far as to be of service to someone or something to the detriment of your chosen career, putting your personal health and livelihood in danger. Gauging and understanding your own limits is always vital. We all have a cutoff point, and the other side of that is your breaking point. It would be wise to learn about how you personally operate by feeling the workings of your body and understanding how far you can push the limits of your onboard surge protector.

Explaining to Pam, that if she were to start her business as a beautician, that it most likely would be a success. If in six months, the business hadn't gone as planned and was not working for her, to then have a look at the positive achievements that she had experienced.

For example: Remembering her clients that she had been of service to, while at the same time, recalling the conversations that she engaged in with people from all walks of life. Within these conversations could possibly hold the key to the next level of her life's journey. That she should honour herself for taking a leap of faith, while at the same time, to not be disheartened that her business didn't go as planned. The point is, Pam followed her downloaded idea and made it happen, as she brought her inspiration through to fruition. I went on to say that she would learn an awful lot about herself, business and people skills, suggesting to flip the coin and look at the situation as a success, signifying that: "when you change the way that you look at things, the things you look at change".

Sometimes we have to go through situations in life to arrive at the next level of our personal journey. We may not always understand what is happening until sometime in the future. Life is full of lessons as we grow within ourselves while moving forward on our life's journey. Never be concerned about the destination. Your destination will show up eventually.

The idea of opening a beautician shop came to Pam as a way to be of service to mankind. An obstacle she had to overcome was the fear of "What if it doesn't work?", and to not listen to someone saying, "Oh, that will never work!" She would have to conquer her fear and trust in herself, placing her faith in the hands of the divine energies by sliding across from the passenger's seat into the driving position, therefore, taking control of her life. This included finding a suitable store location, then setting up the finances to obtain the shop lease and fitting out the store, along with advertising to get her first batch of clients. All the while, Pam would be, in essence, "taking one step at a time" while trusting in herself and placing her faith in the universal energies.

My final words to Pam during our meeting that day were "Don't put your energies into thinking, *What if it doesn't work?* Instead, embrace a productive mindset, believing, *What if it does work?*" Changing the way that you see things opens up the source of positive energies, thereby creating a positive outcome for any given situation.

When we set out to unselfishly be of service to others, the universal energies step in to help make things happen. This is a special kind of magic. As I have said in previous chapters, we always have that nagging question in our minds: *What is my life's purpose?* I believe that we are all born to be the best that we can be, with the skills that we are born with. We can help our fellow man evolve by sharing with them our experiences that we have learned growing within ourselves while living out our earthly existence here on this beautiful planet. This helps our fellow man to learn and develop within themselves. It's a perpetual giving and receiving evolution of mankind.

Too often, we let ourselves be dictated to by those around us. We seem to believe that our peers somehow know and understand what is best for us. Putting yourself in such a situation can be detrimental. When this happens, we are handing over the reins to another driver, choosing to just exist and wait. However, the waiting will never stop as life passes you by. That is until you regain control of your life. There is far more to you than just existing. Nobody on this planet, or any other planet, possess your specific manual to troubleshoot the problems in your life. In fact, you don't have this elusive manual either. If there were such a thing, I put it to you that we write such personal manuals as we progress through our lives.

We were not born without some sort of internal guidance to navigate through our lifetime. In fact, we are all born with our own onboard navigational system. There are senses that we have within us from the day we were born that send information to our brains to help us understand and perceive the world around us. These five primary senses are sight, hearing, smell, taste, and touch. Then we have what most call a "gut feeling" about something or someone. This is known as the sixth sense, called *intuition*. Remember those times when you had a strong feeling about someone or a place that you have entered; perhaps it felt very comfortable, or maybe you had a strong feeling that something just didn't feel right. This is your intuition sending out warning signals, making you aware of your surroundings.

Your senses are an essential tool for you to navigate through your life's journey. Make a start to truly understand and embrace your personal triggers. Make it a personal mission to get to know yourself better than you do now. It's a great idea to start creating a daily journal as you navigate through your life so that you will become much more aware and in tune with yourself, taking one step at a time and savouring those precious moments of your personal realisations as you fine-tune your awareness and happenings around you and within your life situations.

Being productive and on top of your game requires keeping a healthy lifestyle, such as eating the right foods that your body was designed to eat; taking time off from your daily work to recuperate; getting a good night sleep is vital to perform well at all levels. Being proactive and on top of your game requires a sharp mind, so it makes a lot of sense that we eat well, sleep well, and rest well.

As a psychic medium, one must be fit and ready to be of service to one's clients. One must be able to give to one's clients the best reading results possible during their meeting, whether it be a one-on-one reading or in a group reading, while always being prepared. The responsibility of being a psychic medium is not to be taken lightly. It is a huge responsibility that requires a lifetime of dedication. It takes a healthy lifestyle, daily meditation, and continuing education by reputable teachers to further understand and to build on your craft. Therefore, you are always evolving to a higher level, enhancing your gifts and abilities that you were born with, which is always a positive continuous endeavour.

It doesn't matter what specific career you undertake. You may not even be a part of the workforce. Your daily diet is essential to achieving the best results possible with whatever you undertake so that the end result is living a joyous life, without that feeling of sluggishness and fatigue always knocking at your door.

Changing your unhealthy lifestyle to living a more healthy and vibrant lifestyle is achieved by finding teachers who specialise within the specific areas that interest you, taking it all one step at a time. You may not resonate with attending a gym every other day, although you may enjoy taking up a recreational activity that naturally keeps you fit and healthy, such as scuba diving, bicycle riding, nature walks, or surfing, just to name a few.

Step outside your comfort zone. Write down a list of personal achievements on a whiteboard that you would like to achieve over the next twelve months or so while always remembering to live one step at a time, embracing life with undying gratitude.

EPILOGUE

Information from conversations can lead to the validation of your vocation.

—Doc O'Toole

Throughout this book, I have taken you on a journey of discovery, from my life as a singer-songwriter to my present work as a psychic medium. Working with my abilities as a psychic medium has been a pleasure and a gift that I truly honour and cherish, each and every day. I will always continue to be of service to those who need closure, direction, and guidance along their life's journey. I'm no different from anyone else. That is, we all have a title that we work under, which is the only thing that separates us in our chosen fields of service. Though the bottom line is that being of service to others is honouring who we are as we work in parallel with our gifts and abilities that we were born with, no matter what the subject or title that is held.

Recently, I visited my friend, Scott, in hospital, who has a business in finance. During our two-hour conversation, he explained that it is essential for him to educate his clients so that they understand the workings and knowledge of the financial world as they transition through the process of taking out a loan. He ensures that his clients receive the best possible outcome for their financial undertakings.

I already knew how much Scott truly cared for the welfare of his friends, family, and clients, not only in finance but in general. I am always amazed at the level of respect and kindness that Scott shows to his fellow man. No matter how many times we have had these types of conversations, I'm always amazed at the level of respect that

Scott holds for those around him. The best part is that, to Scott, it's healthy and second nature to help others and think to in this way. Understanding and being of service to a high standard is always Scott's primary objective. That's magic happening right there.

So you see, there are many ways to be of service to those around you. The law of attraction and the universal energies always apply to whatever your undertakings may be. We all have a calling of some type, a calling to something that we are uniquely passionate about. There is something deep within us that lights us up, shining through us, in turn igniting our futures, no matter how big or how small that thing maybe. You will inevitably discover this when you dare to take hold of whatever it is you are called to do. The universal energies will partner with you to make sure you have the best outcome possible. The trick here is to have total faith and belief in oneself, to step outside your comfort zone to make it happen while taking it all at a steady pace, all one step at a time.

We are all "students of the universe." While reading through the previous chapters, you will have discovered the universal energies and workings of the universe itself. I too, have discovered these throughout my life so far. At the same time, the light of validation for what you have experienced in your lifetime has hopefully answered those lingering questions within you.

You will begin to understand that, yes, there is more to life as your internal beacon begins to glow brightly, shining through you, illuminating the positive energies that will flow out into the world. It doesn't matter who you are or where you come from or what others may think of you. It also doesn't matter what others think you should be achieving or aspiring to. Always be mindful that we are all born totally as individuals with our own very unique qualities, with one purpose in common, which is to make a difference within the community or farther afield. At the same time, we are always learning and evolving to a higher level so that we can be of greater service to mankind.

As my psychic medium abilities came on strongly in the early nineties, I didn't honestly acknowledge or fully understand what I had. I never fully understood that I could also be of service, helping people with my abilities. However, at times throughout those early days, I did occasionally perform readings for friends and associates who required my assistance with one thing or another, with startling results. Back then, if ever an "odd man out" was needed, it would be me raising my hand to accept that position gleefully.

Accepting my psychic medium abilities was something that I didn't take lightly. Once I had accepted what I had been born to, it took me more than another twelve months to finally own it. I kept questioning my close friend and psychic medium Sonja, "Are you sure that's what I am?"

She became a little frustrated after a while, replying, "Well, you do communicate with spirit, don't you?"

"Yes," I replied.

Sonja responded, in a matter of fact way, "Well, then, you're a medium!"

I actually remember the last time I questioned Sonja, who is highly regarded as a psychic medium herself. I thought *I'd better not ask her that question again. She's becoming a little frustrated with me and my questioning.* So I took the final plunge, fully owning the gift that I was born with. I'm so thankful to Sonja for all she has done for me. Her undying faith in me and my abilities gave me the strength to keep moving forward, trusting in myself, pushing myself forward, learning and honing my skills, week in week out, year after year. So far, owning my abilities and being of service to mankind has lead me on a fantastic journey of self-discovery, travelling overseas, meeting new people while feeling blessed to meet likeminded people along the way. To me, I am so glad that I said yes to my calling, as I often sit in a quiet place reflecting on my clients that I have been able to help and be of service to, sharing my knowledge with them as I deliver messages to them from Spirit.

My friends had always known about my abilities. Yes, they actually knew before I did. Now that I look back and reflect on situations throughout my life, I realise that having a natural gift seemed as healthy as the air we breathe. So I never questioned it and never really looked at it. This is as close as I can come to explaining why I found it hard to see what I had been born with.

From the time I accepted, I am a psychic medium, the universal energies opened up, even more, helping me and landing me in situations of learning, travelling, attending courses, public speaking, and attending workshops both in Australia and overseas. I increasingly began performing one-on-one readings both privately and at a spiritual store, known as Krystal Kamali, which also included the occasional group readings, which I love to do. I look forward to increasing group readings in the near future.

Little by little, one step at a time, I began to grow stronger as I studied books, listening to podcasts along with online research of known mediums that I discovered in my surfing travels on the internet. I became very focused, applying myself to study and research, as I still do to this very day. It is highly relevant to study and understand the mechanics of mediumship, for when you acknowledge and accept this type of work, you are also taking on considerable responsibility. People are always searching for guidance and answers in their lives, whether they need closure after losing a loved one who has crossed over or needs validations and guidance to see them to the next level within their lives. I always light up internally when I am performing a reading for a client. It is so rewarding to be the lighthouse for another human being. It is even more rewarding to see my clients sail off into the distance as they traverse the now calm waters into their next life's adventure, no longer carrying the burden they lugged around with them months before.

Throughout the chapters in this book, I have shared some stories that can help you transition forward to the next step in your personal journey. Hopefully, I have shared this well so that you can also tap into your own natural-born abilities, which we all have from the day that we entered this world. Trusting in your personal skills is a big thing. That's why I have mentioned meditation numerous times throughout the previous chapters, suggesting you begin the modality of meditation daily.

The practice of meditation is very beneficial to your daily lifestyle. Employing this skill as a part of your daily rituals will keep you grounded, giving you a greater sense of self-awareness, reducing the anxiety and stresses of everyday life, which in turn invokes within you greater clarity, helping you to obtain a stronger focus in all your endeavours while encouraging a healthy connection between your mind, body, and soul.

I meditate daily before leaving my home in the morning. I call it the "Seat Belt to life". Sometimes, I will sit in silence for at least twenty minutes. Other times, I start off my meditation with breathwork, breathing in through the nose and out through the mouth. I then ground myself by imagining divine chords attached to the base of my spine and souls of my feet as I imagine the divine chords going down deep into the earth, held there by a lightning rod. I then take all my negativity, down through my divine chords, deep into the ground, transmuting the negative energies into positive energies. I then bring up all the transmuted energies and the earth's healing energies up into my body, creating inner light, inner shine, inner peace, inner courage, and so forth. I then say prayers for people in need of help or for families dealing with a disease. You can use this meditation for yourself or use it as a guide to creating the meditation that resonates with you. Usually, my morning meditation takes about fifteen minutes, although I sometimes do it in five minutes when I am running late.

If you have any doubts about your purpose in life, even though you have been prompted internally to act on a specific idea, the universal energies will bring situations and conversations in line with your doubts and questions. This is also known as "signs and symbols." These validate whether to move on an idea or not. Begin today by starting to build your faith within you while remembering that you are a student of the universe, that we all have a specific purpose in life.

Your life's purpose will show up at precisely the right time. However, throughout your life, while living and wondering, *What is my life's purpose?* You are already on the road to your ultimate life's purpose. The path that you are on can be viewed as the apprenticeship road. You will know when you have completed your apprenticeship, and that will be the day that you begin to do what really lights you up inside.

"Passion drives you, we don't drive our passion".

–Doc O'Toole

ACKNOWLEDGMENTS

I feel very blessed to be writing this book and would like to thank the divine help and support from God, Archangel Michael, my Spirit guides, and the universal energies for their continued guidance.

Thank you for the chance meeting with a medium over a meal that set me on this journey. During a very general conversation, the medium, who I will call Joy, all of a sudden switched the discussion, and within the next breath said to me, "You have to write books." It took me a few seconds to readjust my thoughts from a general conversation to mediumship, as I realised that Joy had been chosen to deliver me a message. I sat there in amazement, looking back and forward at Joy and at the figure that now appeared beside her.

There had been a prominent figure whom I saw quite clearly standing next to Joy, who passed a few years before as she was giving me a reading that intensely validated what she had been conveying. I was absolutely floored with who I was seeing as I put down my knife and fork to negotiate within my mind what was suddenly taking place. I had mentioned to Joy a few times throughout the impromptu reading, "Do you know who is standing next to you?" I also mentioned the name of the spirit energy standing there, but Joy, as it seemed, never heard a word I said. Thus, began the first step towards writing this book.

At the Hay House Writer's Workshop in Sydney a month after my impromptu reading, I had been in the foyer walking around looking at all the stands of books that were on display. I happened upon Balboa Press. I didn't know what they were all about, but they invited me to be on their mailing list. I said, "Sure, why not?"

That following September after the Hay House Writer's Workshop, I received a phone call from Balboa Press, asking what my book was about. Thinking on my feet, I went on to discuss my thoughts on what I would like to write about for the benefit of mankind. One hour later, I was signed to Balboa Press.

- To the appearance of the prominent figure, as mentioned above and to the medium, Joy, I thank you.

- To the team of Balboa Press and Hay House, thank you for all that you continue to do in this world and for the continuous support that I personally experienced throughout the writing process, right from the beginning of this project.

- To Sonja, thank you for your continued support, always believing in me and my abilities and for hiring me as a reader all those years ago. I had no idea where this journey would lead me. Wow!

- To Rod P, for being my accountability partner throughout the writing process. Most of all, for your loyalty and support throughout the entire development.

- To Rod and Liza Davidson, Walter, Nida and John, Karen and Donald, Mary K, Caroline and Ty, Janet P (NJ), Luke and Carol, Sue S, Robyn C, Sue K, Daphne (NJ), Jocelyn and Theo (MA), Petra and Mike, James DP, and TJ Jackson. To Jody and the team of Krystal Kamali. The list goes on. Without the support and well-wishes of friends and associates, this book wouldn't have happened, as it takes more than one person to write a book.

- To my clients and those who have shared their stories for this book, from the bottom of my heart, I thank you.

- To John Holland, thank you for all that you do as a psychic medium. Thank you for your kind words of wisdom and support, along with your teaching skills and compassion that you share with the world.

- To Brian Robertson, Christine Morgan, Simon James, it was an absolute pleasure being a student of "Into the Mist."

- To the psychic mediums and spiritual teachers whose teachings I have had the privilege to be a part of as a student, thank you for your knowledge and all that you continue doing.

- Finally, to Karen Geraghty. I cannot thank you enough for your love and support. I'm so glad that I told you before you passed away about the planned surprise of dedicating this book to you in honour of your unwavering love and support. I miss you and love you, eternally.

ABOUT THE AUTHOR

Working as a psychic medium since 2013, Doc O'Toole has been aware of his abilities for far longer, as he now devotes his life to his calling. While he continues to learn and hone the skills that of a psychic medium, he has travelled as far as the USA on a few occasions to attend the John Holland Advanced Mediumship Workshops while also attending workshops in Australia, namely "Into the Mist" with Brian Robertson, Christine Morgan, and Simon James. Performing as a public speaker on the occasional requests, Doc enjoys sharing his psychic medium knowledge to enlighten those in need of direction. Working one on one with his clients with the occasional group readings, he is very passionate and caring throughout the reading process as he delivers messages from Spirit.

Contact the author at: www.psychicmedium.rocks.

Printed in the United States
By Bookmasters